QUEEN OF SHEEBA

MIRIAM ROBINSON

DORRANCE
PUBLISHING CO
EST. 1920
PITTSBURGH, PENNSYLVANIA 15238

Dorrance Publishing Co
585 Alpha Drive
Pittsburgh, PA 15238
Visit our website at www.dorrancebookstore.com

ISBN: 979-8-8868-3085-9
eISBN: 979-8-8868-3945-6

DEDICATION TO THE LONEY AND THOMAS FAMILY

I wrote this book to let my families know that I am a well trained Christian young woman, a homemaker, a retired Production Controller for the United States Navy (Civil Service), a widow, a Seminary and College Graduate and Financial Business Person, or even yet a potent Missionary Agency among our people as is the Theologians, and I claim that at the present stage of our development in the South I am more important and necessary.

INTRODUCTION

The material in this book had been presented to provide the Black Woman with the basic tools with which to begin to consciously regenerate consciousness on the personal social, and planetary levels.

Once she has truly grasped the fundamentals, she can create her own process according to the stories of messengers. There are countless effective processes that may be created, utilized, and shared with other women. As long as she is in tune with the intent of extended harm her of getting necessities would be over. After looking at harm positions of several hundred women, we study the strategies used to get the top position (principal or main woman).

In the scripture (1 Kings 10:1-13) more light should have been shredded on her because she helped King Solomon to reach his goals. In (2 Chronicles 4:28-31; 9:1-9, 12) the writers of the King James Bible from Oxford University didn't shed very much light about the Queen of Sheba's amounts given to King Solomon, helping him to take Jerusalem to its highest height in history, Ethiopia and Tyree were omitted which he made a chronological order of credit to the nearby provinces. It was intended to glorify Solomon rather than give information about this wealthy Queen, which is otherwise spoken very little in the Old and New Testament Bibles.

In the Chronicles, the provinces were as follows: Bee-sheba, Moladah, Hazar-Shual, Bilhah, Elem, Tolad, Bethuel, Hormah, Ziklag, Beth-Marcaboth, Hazar-Susim, Beth-Birel, and Shaaraim.

Even during King David's reign, Ethiopia and Hiram of Tyree were supplying Jerusalem with the necessaries and considered to have been hi principle carriers (1 Kings 5:3), Hiram formed the same alliance with Solomon he had with King David, his dad.

This book also claims its greatness, for it must be legit. If it weren't for the text it would have suppressed the Europeans and Africa alike, nor would it have languished in the British museum for over seventy years. In fact, the Zagues (Kings of Ethiopia), who were in the Solomonic Line, were themselves suppressors of the books. So far more than a thousand years this history of Ethiopia has awaited the readership it desires.

CONTENTS

Queen of Sheba

The Queen of Sheba and Tribes

1000-700 B.C.

Genealogies

Cush, Ham, and Japheth (Genesis 9:18)

Cush
Nemroid

12th Century (Assyria w. Arabia) Oresent Hejaz

Queen of Sheba (in Mariaba, Capital Home Arabia)

Menelik (Sheba's only son)

1200 B.C.   Southward migration of Sheba and related Tribes
1000 B.C.   Great expansion of Sheba power
800 B.C.   Known Priestly Kings of Sheba
450 B.C.   Sheba Changed to Monarchy
400 B.C.   Kingdoms to Main (Minaeans) and Quataban flourished

Abraham
    Noah
    Ahem
    David
    Solomon
    Menelik and Rehoboam

QUEEN OF SHEBA'S HOMETOWN, LOCATION AND POPULATION

ETHIOPIA

Critically speaking, Ethiopia, now known as Nubia, which was once the Sudan. It is 75 times larger than Israel. The country farther west and South is Southern Abyssinia. The settled population was small, since in ancient as in modern Egypt naturally drew away most of the able-bodies and energetic youth as servants, police and soldiers, and a territory smaller than Egypt and excluding deserts smaller than Belgium. The prehistoric population of Northern Nubia was probably Egyptian but this was replaced in historic time by a Black race, tall, muscular and commanding people by a Black race, and the thick lips and black wooly and straight-haired descendant of Cush. Typical Africans are as well marked in the oldest Egyptian paintings as in the latest. The artist says pure Negro Stock has been mixed with the fellaheen of Egypt and with the Seminite population of the Arabian Coast. The rulers of Ethiopia were generally of reign blood. The Negroes, though brave and frugal, were slow in thought, which the Arabians thought, and although controlled for centuries by cultivated neighbors, under whom they attained at times high official prominence, yet the body of a people remained uninfluenced by this civilization. The country, which was now known as Abyssinia, was largely controlled, from the earliest known date, by a Caucasian people who had crossed the Red Sea from Arabia. The true Abyssinians, as Professor Littmann shows, contains no Negro Blood and no Negro qualities; in general they are "well formed and handsome, with straight and regular features, lively eyes, hair long and straight or somewhat curled and in color, dark olive approaching brown." Modern discoveries prove their close racial and linguistic connection with Southern Arabia and some writers think that the Cushities resemble the Egyptians particularly with the Kingdom of Sheba (the Sabaeans) that powerful people whose extensive architectural and literary remains have recently come to light. The Sabaeans' inscriptions found in Abyssinia go back some 2600 years and give a new value to the bible reference as well as to the constant claim of Jos, that the Queen of Sheba was a "queen of Ethiopia." The Falashas are a Jewish Community living near Lake Tsana, of the same physical type and probably of the same race as Abyssinians. Their religion is a "pure Mossism" based upon the Ethiopic version of the Rent, but modified by the fact they are ignorant of the Hebrew language Tew Enc. It is certain when they became Jews. The older scholars thought of them as dating back to the Solomonic era, or at least to Babylonia capacity. Since the researchers of Joseph Harvey 1868, some date within the Christian area has seem preferable. Not withstanding their ignorance of the Talmudic rules. However, the newly discovered fact that a strong Jewish Community was flourishing in Syene in the six century B.C. makes it clear that Jewish influence may have been felt in Ethiopia at least that early. Although Abyssinians are noted for their strict adherence to ancient customs, Jewish traditions were practiced all round the entire country. The opening formula of the King in every official letter "the Loin of the Tribe of Judah has been conquered" is no more Jewish than scores of ordinary phrased and customs. Although it is barely possible that some rites, like circumcision and observance of the Sabbath, may have been received from the ancient Egyptians or Christians cops (New Sch-Herz Enc.) yet a strong Hebrew influence cannot be denied. All travelers speak of the industry of the Falashas and the "kindliness and grave courtesy" of the Abyssinians. Besides those named above, there are many communities of mixed races in Ethiopia but the ancient basis is invariably Negro, Seminite or Egyptian.

HISTORY

The ancient Greek writers were full of fantastic and fabulous stories about Ethiopia. Sometimes they became so puzzled in; their geography as to speak of Ethiopia as extending as far as India; their notes concerning the miraculous "fauna and flora" are equally Manchurian. Homer praised the Ethiopians as being a "blameless race", and other writers rank them first among all men for their religious knowledge. This latter notion may have had its origin from a priesthood—which had the power of and death over kings—as the divinely ordained primitive custom, or it may have sprung from the fact that the Egyptian "Land of the Gods" was partly situated on Southern Abyssinia. It is suggested that the Hebrew prophets never fell into these common errors but invariably "gave a very good idea of geographical and political conditions" (W. Max Muller). The oldest important historic document referring to Ethiopia is from the 4th dynasty of Egypt when Sneferue laid waste the land, capturing 7,000 slaves and 100,000 cattle. In the 6th dynasty the Egyptians reached as far South as the Second Cataract and brought back some dwarfs, but did not establish any permanent control. In the 12th dynasty Egypt's real occupation of Ethiopia began. Usertesen III records his contempt by saying "The Negro obeys as the lips are open. They are miserable, both tails and bodies", not withstanding this satiric reference, these naked Ethiopians clad in skins and tails of wild animals, compelled the Pharaoh to make several campaigns before he could establish a frontier at the 2nd Cataract beyond which no Negro could come without a permit. That the natives were not cowardly may be seen from the songs of triumph over their subjection from the fact that everyone later was encouraged by the Pharaoh to enlist in his army, until finally the very hieroglyphics for archers became a Nubian issue. The 18th dynasty pushed the frontier beyond the 3rd Cataract into the splendid Dongola District and often boasts of the rich tribute from Ethiopia.

The chairs of ivory and the jewelry sometimes shown seem barbaric in style but excellent in workmanship, copper and bronze factories and great iron foundries dated also to a very early time in Ethiopia, the Ethiopian gold mines, where hundreds of criminals toiled with ears and noses mutilated. In Egypt in the 15th century B.C. as "common as dusk", the choice son of Pharaoh, next to him in power was proud to be called "Prince of Cush". Amenhotep IV (1370 B.C.) the religious reformer built his second greatest temple (the only one of his works is now in existent) in Nubia. The 19th dynasty sought to colonize Ethiopia, and some of the most magnificent temples ever built by man can be seen as far south as the 4th cataract. For over five centuries, Egyptian rule was maintained until about 1000 B.C. A war for independence began, which was so successful that the victorious Ethiopian Kings finally carried their armies against Thebes and Memphis and for a century (763-663) ruled all Egypt from Napata—which in religious architecture base the Southern Thebes and for another century (and even at times during the Ptolemaic era) controlled upper Egypt. While the leaders of this revolution were doubtless descendants of exile priests from Thebes, yet the mixture of Ethiopian blood is plainly discernible and is perhaps also shown in their "puritan morals". Shabaka=So. (715-707) Tarbarka=(693-667), both were mentioned in the Bible, were the last great kings of Ethiopia. Though the Romans held a nominal protectorate over Ethiopia, it was so little important as to be scarcely ever to be mentioned. After being expelled from Egypt the Ethiopians still continued to honor the gods of Thebes, but, as foreign influence ceased, the representations of this worship became more and more African and barbaric. Even after Christianity had triumphed everywhere else, the Nubians, as late as the 5th century A.D., a native king, Silko, established a Christian Kingdom in the Northern Sudan with Dongola as its capital. This raised somewhat the culture of the land. In the next century the Arabs made Nubia tributary, though it took an immense army to do it. For six centuries thereafter Islam demanded a tribute of 360 slaves annually, and treasures, though innumerable campaigns were necessary to collect it. The Nubian Kings refused all overtures to become Moslems, and the Christian Churches multiplied along the Nile. In the 8th century, Egypt was invaded by 1,000,000 Nubians to repay an insult to the Coptic patriarch and to the sacred pictures in the Egyptian Christian Churches. In the 13th century, David, King of Nubia, not only without tribute but invades Egypt. He was terribly punished, however, by the Arabs, who sacked Churches and tortures Christians clear to the 4th cataract. This was the beginning to the end. By the close of the 15th century, almost every Christian altar was desolate and every Church destroyed.

What every Black child should know is that Africa is four times the size of the United States and three times the size of Europe.

Africa was the pillar of advanced technology and superior civilizations. Cities such as Jene and Timbuktu were the Mecca of intellectual centers that boasted mathematicians, astronomers (Sheba was a the center of astronomical wisdom, worshiping the sun and moons gods), architects physicians and other sciences. African civilizations charted the stars, built the pyramids, created written languages, established the calendar and we now know it and developed networks of world trade as early as 4000 B.C. Many writers called Africa the Cradle of Humanity.

Tribal wars and slave trade were the primary reason that brought the depopulation and downfall of the Africa States. It is documented that the Afro-European slave trade began 1441 at the hands of the Portuguese, and later joined by the Spanish, French, Dutch and English as slave traders. The first slaves were reported in English America 1607, as "Black Gold" and the beasts of burden. Europeans established trading posts along the West African Coastlines where beads, guns, whiskey, and Ivory were exchanged for African slaves (Orr 1915).

ANIMAL LIFE

Among the animals peculiar to Africa are the buffalo, two horned rhinoceros, hippopotami, zebras, gorillas, Quagga, gnu, giraffes, hyenas, deer, aardwolves, many species of monkeys elephants, crocodiles, alligators, fish, insects, flies, locusts, myth, bees, scorpions and ants.

SOCIAL CONDITIONS

Now the social conditions of Africa are in the state of flux. Polygamy and slavery are still found in some area. Life there is more or less savage. There is an absence of central authority, and many of the people are fettered with terror and superstition. While European occupation is gradually bettering social conditions through employment and education, remote sections were constantly populated by savage and semi-civilized conditions are grumbling before the advance of European enterprise.

PARTITION

The position of African has been going on for several decades and various spheres of the influence have been fixed. Great Britain, France, Italy, Belgium, Spain, and Portugal have established colonies in or claim protectorates over more than three fourth of the continent, while France had the largest area. Great Britain holds the most valuable possessions, due to the fact that Britain territory is more fertile and had a climate more favorable to industrial and commercial development. Germany and Turkey lost their former extensive territories as a result of World War I; those holdings were taken over chiefly as protectorates and now are under the governments of Belgium, Italy, France, and Great Britain (Hendelson 1955).

ETHIOPIA

In the very north were the Aglow people, to the north were the Caucasoid; in the southeast were the Bushmanoids. In the south of Arabia were the Hasbushas (Semities, Caucasoids spoke Cushitic Languages, others spoke Gueezl. In 3,000 B.C. the Negroid people pushed into the Pleau from the west introducing agriculture to the Cushites and interbreeding with them.

The Aglow people were the most creative people in all of Africa. They established Ethiopia as an important center of plant domestications, and they maintained intermittent contact with ancient plants and animals with them.

From 1,000 B.C.-400B.C. Semitic speaking people had migrated from South Arabia. They introduced irrigation systems for climate and vegetation. They kept their ancient tribal names, or which Hasbashat made use of metals, the camels and incense, the art of writing techniques of building construction, and the larger scale of political organization.

The ruins of one such city was discovered at Ava, including monoliths, a temple to the sound god and Himgaritic inscriptions dating from the 7th to the 5th century. The elaborate of the Semities' ruins were also found at Axum in Tyree, which was the center of a city-state founded before the beginning of the Christian era. There is one obelisk that remains standing; the others were in ruins beneath the modern city. Axumite dominions are the ruins of the temples and town. Steles and obelisks, and reservoirs and dams, which were a testament to the cultural aspects of those people, who were to leave their imprint on Ethiopian history (Simon 1960).

HOW THE QUEEN WAS
DISCOVERED
(FICTION)

There was a magic worked by the devil, and she was a pretty Abyssinian girl. She was walking, when she saw a dragon coming near her, so quickly she hid in the branches of a tree. Now this same dragon was seen and executed by some holy men, some Ethiopian saints they were. Justice, the dragon died, and a drop of the dragon's blood dripped on the foot of that girl. Once it touched her, her foot turned into a cloven hoof. Now when she returned to her village, it became known that the dragon was dead, and the people honored the girl for killing it. Little that they knew, she was not the one responsible for its death, but mistaken people made her their Queen. The wood of the tree of paradise blessed the Queen of Sheba, but it did not heal her cloven foot. King David said, "God reigned in the wood." And that's how she came to be known as the Queen of Sheba—Sheba, which was the country of her birth (Housman 1997).

Solomon would not permit such ungodliness to pass before his eyes. He healed her himself when she stepped over the thread hold of the palace. It was a miracle.

The queen's stories have been embellished by Muslim Commentators the Arabs gave her a Southern Arabian genealogy, and she is the subject of a wide spread of legends (Mc Cullif 1999).

HOOPOE BIRD

According to one account, Solomon, having heard from a Hoopoe, one of his birds, that she (Bilquis) and her kingdom worshipped the sun and the moon, he sent her a letter asking her to worship God. She replied by sending gifts, but when Solomon proved unreceptive to them, she went to his court herself. The Hoopoe also whispered to him that she had very hairy legs and the hooves of an ass. Solomon, being curious about such a peculiar phenomenon, had a glass floor built before his throne so that Bilquis, tricked into thinking it was water, raised her skirts to cross it and revealed that her legs in fact were truly hairy. Solomon then ordered his demons to create a depilatory for the queen (Safra 1998).

The hoopoe is a beautiful with a disgusting habit: it probes foul places for insects with its sharp, slender beak. Its wing feathers bear a zebra stripe, and its head sports a lovely crown of feathers. When frightened, the hoopoe may flutter his chest or drop to the ground and play dead. The offensive order picked up from its feeding grounds is enough to drive away most of its enemies.

Called lapwing in the KJV, the hoopoe is on the list of unclean birds (Leviticus 11:19; Deuteronomy 14:18). It is frequently seen throughout the Holy Land today (Nelson 1995).

SOLOMON'S WIVES AND CONCUBINES (970 B.C.)

(1 Kings 3:1)	Principle Wife, childless, she was the Pharaoh's daughter of Egypt, and her name was Lady Tanis. Because she was without a house of her own, Solomon built her an expensive near his. She was more interested in the horses than the soldiers, linen, yarn, or the town of Gazer, where the Canaanites lived. She died before Solomon
(1 Kings 10:1-13)	The Queen of Sheba (Madeka) as Pre-Islamic, for Allah was her God. From Ethiopia and Egypt, she brought spices, gold, and precious stones. Polygamy made the position of the chief precarious, and at ant time the king might capriciously promote

over her head some of her rivals however, she gave birth to Solomon's first son Menelik.

(1 Kings 11:1)   Many women of the Moabites Chemnosh was their goddess

(1 Kings 11:1)   Many of Solomon's wives were Ammonites, Milcom and Molech were their Goddess. One was named Naamah, the Granddaughter of King Nabash. One of those wives of that group gave birth to Solomon's second son, Rehoboam, who succeeded king Solomon in 931-913 B.C. He became King at 41 years old.

(1 Kings 11:1)   For the women of the Edomites, Hudad was their goddess. Esau sold his birthright. Herod was a true one Limestone, porphyry, sandstone, copper, volcano stones, wheat, figs, pomegranates, and olives were plentiful.

(1 Kings 11:1)   For the women of Zidonians, Ashtoreth and Baal were their goddesses. Fish and cedar wood were plentiful. Jezebel's father a King of Zid.

(1 Kings 11:1)   Women of the Hittites had the goddesses Kheta, Hatti, and Kelerous.

(1 Kings 11:1)   Many women of the Phoenicians worshiped Ashtart as their goddess. From Tyre, plenty of cedar, coal and dif ferent woods were plentiful.

700 wives and 300 concubines

2 sons

Solomon wrote 3,000 Proverbs and 1,005 Songs

(Langbaum 1989)

Solomon's main or principle wife was Pharaoh's daughter and he established a relationship with the neighboring people. Hittites and Zidonians were forbidden to Israelites. All of his wives were from wealthy powerful citizen homes to establish his position.

Deuteronomy 7:1-3 says that all foreign nations are greater and mightier than Israel, the Lord thy God shall deliver them and utterly destroy them, thou shall make no covenant with them. Neither shall make marriages with them: thy daughter shall not give his son, nor his daughter shall thou take unto thou son.

1 Kings 10: 15,27 deals with the direct imports and the results of the slaves of silver, cedar and wood became very plentiful in the capital. The visit of Queen Sheba would point to the overload caravan routes from the Yemen being open; Solomon had the merchantmen working the water traffic from Arabia and of the governors of the country.

I and II Kings were drawn from the "annals of the kings of Israel" and was only a section from that literature closer analysis of these books has shown that the larger theological purpose, namely to determine more by their faithfulness to God than the extent of their wealth and the size of their armies (1 Kings 15:20) (II Kings 10:34, 13:8).

Solomon's daughters were married to his own officers. 1 Chronicles 22:14 says Solomon started his reign with a capital sum of 100,000 talents (1 Talent = $60.00) of gold and 1,000,000 talents of silver, a sum greater than the natural debt of Great Britain. This huge sum was ear marked for the building of the temple (Orr 1915).

I wondered why the Queen of Sheba's hometown and Hiram's hometown in Tyree were not mentioned in the Chronicles when King Solomon did his chronological order of cities and towns.

The books of the Chronicles were largely a recasting of I and II Kings, done in an effort to assent the importance of the temple in Jerusalem, and in general to claim priority over the north in religious matters (Zondervan 1997).

Female clans had matriarchal practices, and matrilineal inheritance of ancient Arabia and surrounding countries, in Assyria the head of the family was the female called the "Shebu". Polyandry was sanctioned; a woman could marry as many husbands as she wished, even ready made husbands left their families to live with her. She could divorce either one at anytime. Patriarchy—before this woman were an equal footing with men.

Queen Makeda's tomb along with twenty obelisks of her period were excavated at Axum in the early 1900s and taken to Cairo, Egypt. The rein of Queen Madeka was one of the most beautiful and richest culture and history (Empak Publishing Company).

MARRIAGES AND CONCUBINES

Marriage for life is the social structure, which God deemed best for the human race. It has always-presented problems but it was worked tremendously well.

Throughout the Biblical period, the marriage of a man and a woman appears to be a normal condition for adult life. There were some people who did not marry, and in some cased celibacy (living together, shacking-up, or doubtful) was even recommended (1 Corinthian 7,8,9) for those so gifted. For most people, the needs of love, companionship, sexual satisfaction and the drive to reproduce led them to the state of marriage. Its benefits far outweighed its drawbacks.

Coupling was so normative in a society that a social stigma was attached to those who did not marry. In some circles there was suspicion that those who chose to remain single possessed physical or mental defects or practiced a deviant lifestyle. Indeed, the single woman found her social and official contact seriously limited.

Paul's acceptance of both the single and the married helped remove that stigma for some. The solitary life of Jesus proved marriage was not absolutely necessary for a full life (Matthew 22:30) and could be enjoyed thoroughly. Despite the frequent exceptions, matrimony was the rule for the contended majority.

Over the centuries the family structure changed with shifting values, but the basic elements of lifetime partnerships general remained the same.

POLYGAMY

Polygamy is the practice of having more than one wife and appears to have been widely accepted in the ancient time. Many leading and Godly men were polygamous. Not only did the practice exist in time of King David and his son Solomon.

This does not mean that polygamy was common among most of the population "simple economies" would have prevented the common man from attempting to support more than one wife. It also does not mean that the Bible prescribes such arrangements. However, the abundance of multiple relationships is obvious. The practice was frequent enough to cause God to offer rules to relate it (Deuteronomy 21:15-17; Exodus 21:10).

In a few cases, a polygamist relationship may actually have been ordered by the scriptures, as in the stance of the Levite marriage (Deuteronomy 25:5-10). Here a man was expected to marry his brother's widow with no question of his current marital status. The widow was theoretically maintaining the relationship with the deceased husband, which was his brother.

We find several reasons which led men to take more than one wife. Some did it because of their cultural strong demand for children. This is why Abraham took Hagar, the Egyptian maid in (Genesis 16:3). It is interesting that Sarah made the suggestion. Documents were discovered at Nuzi, a Mesopotamian City and imply this arrangement was dictated by custom. A second reason was the drive of love; Jacob was trapped and close to take Rachel as a second wife rather than loose her altogether (Genesis 29:18). A third reason is exemplified by King David (2 Samuel 5: 13-16) and Solomon (1 Kings 11:1-3) who married to seal political alliances and gain and to gain political advantages.

Polygamy still existed in Israel during the time of Christ (Herod the great is reported to have had nine wives at once). Conservative religious leaders protected its practice in Jerusalem during this time; by probably many officials had two or more wives. As in other area of daily living, habits and religious rules, we do not see Israelites in agreement regarding polygamy. When a man weighed the possibility of taking more than one wife, he had several things to consider. More wives might provide him with more children, companionship, love, and a larger work force. However, they also would create added expenses, jealousy, and angry relatives. Ironically, the Hebrew word for a second wife means "rival" or "hostile".

A search for a passage, which unequivocally condemns polygamy, reveals that restrictions were placed only on kings (Deuteronomy 17:17). However, several verses suggested that God intention for marriage was one husband and one wife, one flesh (Genesis 2:24). This clear formula is confirmed by Christ (Matthew 19:6; Mark 10:8), showing that polygamy is not a Christian ideal.

The problem of polygamy, a woman having more than one husband, does not seem to be evident among the Jews.

Concubines at the times other women became a part of a family and had a conjugal relationship which the male being the head of the home. Though not wives, they did enjoy a degree of social status. Normal concubines were taken from the slave and poor class. Their roles approximately will remind a person of a modern day mistress. In most cases the concubine was taken for sex and to produce children, especially boys.

Having several such women was a common practice for men who could afford them during the time of the early father until the beginning of the kingdom. Concubines were seen often in the scriptures during the times of the judges.

Some concubines were captured during wartime. Others were Hebrew slaves, gifts from wealthy men or other kings, or children of poverty stricken families. If a concubine was Jewish, she was often treated with respect and her children could become equal heir with the children of the wife. However, gentile concubines were often ignored or abused by other members of the family.

Sometimes it was difficult to discern if a woman in the family actually was a second wife or a concubine. The owner of a concubine in (Judges 19) is called a husband.

The law issues guidelines on concubine's protection. This may not indicate approval of the practice but merely attempt to maintain order (Exodus 21:7-11) and (Deuteronomy 21:10-14) guarantee concubine rights.

Concubines became a way of life among many of Israel's leading figures. No lesser than Jacob, Gideon, Saul, David, Solomon, and Rehoboam had concubines.

In the Bible, Solomon possessed the most concubines. He collected 700 wives of royal birth and 300 concubines (1 Kings 11:3), a figure that is mathematically staggering, but possible nevertheless. Many ancient kings assembled harems of enormous sizes. Not only did they give pleasure to Solomon, but also helped him to produce more children for the kingdom. It was impossible to redefine those ladies as housecleaners of governess; they were clearly designated as concubines. The multiple wives were evidently part of peace treaties made countries of their origin, while the concubines may often have been gifts; in humility it would be best to admit that we do not entirely understand such situation. God certainly supports the one wife marriage; however, he obviously allowed David to keep his "master's wives" (1 Samuel 12:8).

Solomon's life was spiritually eroded by his pagan wives who turned his head toward idolatry (1 Kings 11:4), yet Solomon did much good, for he maintained peace in Israel or 40 years. It is interesting to note that when Solomon wrote his passionate love song to Tirzah, the Shulamite woman, he already had 60 wives and 80 concubines (Song of Solomon 6:8,9).

Dowry—there were ways in which gifts might exchange hands as a dowry. The groom might pay the father of the bride for the lost value of his daughter. A present might be given from a father to the son or daughter.

The first might be a sizeable gift to the father. (Genesis 29:18) Jacob and Rachael (1 Samuel 18:25) gave an outrageous gift of Michael to David hoping he would be killed

The second might be a sizeable gift to the departing daughter. In some cases during the time of Christ, 10 % of the dowry was spent on luxuries for the bride. This guaranteed her enough to purchase perfumes, jewelry, and sometimes false teeth. The Pharaoh gave his daughter Tanis the devastated city of Gezer, as a present to her, when she married Solomon (1 Kings 9:16), he shrewdly rebuilt the city.

The third might be exchanged between the bride and groom, like Rebecca and her husband to be, Isaac (Genesis 24:53). This practice persisted into the first century A.D. (Coleman 1984).

CANDACE AND SHEBA

(Acts 8:27) Many secular monuments speak of high honor paid to woman in Ethiopia. Candace, who went to Jerusalem to worship, had charge of all her jewelry and treasure, which was found by Ferlini in 1824. Now her picture and her jewelry can be seen in Kaga, in the British Museum.

(Genesis 10:1-10; Isaiah 43:3) Again and again the recent discovery Sabaen inscriptions throughout Abyssinia corroborated the relationship.

(1 Kings 10:1-10) The Queen of Sheba heard of Solomon, for it was evident that she was a Black biblical figure.

(Ezekiel 27:22) The merchants of Sheba and Raamah. They were merchants. They occupied in fairs with chiefs of all spices, precious stones, and gold.

(Ps 72:15) And he shall live, and to him shall be given of gold of Sheba: prayer also shall be made for him continually; and daily shall he be praised.

(2 Chronicles 9 1-12 The Queen of Sheba propounded riddles, which the wise king solved them; she was so amazed that she conceded, "the haft has not been told".

(Matthew 12:42) Jesus reproving the Scribes and Pharisees for demanding a sign, told them of the visit of the "Queen of the South" and that "one greater than Solomon" was even in their presence (Coleman 1984).

BRIGHT HISTORY OF (I AND II KINGS)

A set of passages that rely on the association with Africans as a way to establish the positive status of a biblical character is the fourth told reference to Solomon marrying the "Daughter of Pharaoh". In the first instance (1 Kings 3:1), the mention of the marriage comes on the heels of the notice that the kingdom was established in the hands of Solomon (2:46b). The impression is that the marriage is one the first notice (1 Kings 9:16) is a parenthetical interpolation into the details of this territory. Interestingly, the notice is in conjunction with a mention of Egyptian military might and of the fact that Pharaoh gives conquered territory to Solon as part of his daughter's dowry. The third notice of the marriage (1 Kings 9:24) is used to illustrate Solomon's wealth and building activities, while in the fourth instance (1 Kings 11:1) the marriage begins the list of foreign wives in the Deuteronomic negative evaluation of Solomon.

Most researchers have concentrated on the identification of the Pharaoh who made such an alliance with Solomon. They also noted that while the practices of the Egyptian Pharaohs were to consolidate their power thorough political marriages, this always occurred through their sons and through their daughters. In fact the Amarna Letters attest to the fact that such marriage as the one credited to Solomon were forbidden. Surely such was known to the readers of the day. Thus, one must ask what function is served by having such notices of Solomon marrying an Egyptian Princess (Gray 1970).

Some writers made a twofold claim on Solomon and Sheba's marriage. On the other hand, the writers are making the claim not only Solomon adopted the governing practices of the Egyptians, political alliance through intermarriage, but also that he was able to achieve what other nations could not, in this instance the marriage to an Egyptian Princess. Therefore, Solomon's esteem was raised through this association. He could achieve the impossible. On the other hand, he was portrayed as one who took the Egyptian model and perfected it; in other words, he played the game better than they did. Thus this was a fourfold notice of Solomon's diplomatic genius. This is especially seen when all of his wives listed with their nationalities; Sheba was listed in terms of gentile relationship (Sheffield Press 87 &1990).

BLACKS IN THE BIBLE

The heaviness lies on the historical question of the visit and the visitor. Solomon lived by his word; his life spoke on his behalf balanced the readiness of his mouth so that his down and rising up, his table, his law, his work, his love, and his life were alone. Those to whom he gave orders felt that his words were kind and those who committed faults were admonished gently. Solomon's house was built upon wisdom of God and his father. Solomon smiled graciously on fools and to the wise he said parables that had the sweetness of honey.

Solomon, I think as the wisest man that ever lived and was able to put his gear in the high scoring position, passing the test of African riddles and wisdom. Most writers seem to think this was the most different test to be posted. The African queen states: the report was true which I heard in my own land of your affairs and of your wisdom, but I did not believe the reports until I came and with my own eyes had seen it; and behold, the half was not told to me: your wisdom and prosperity surpass the report which I heard. To the ancient reader that speech was seen as true validation if Solomon as the wise and prosperous king. This places an Israel king above African wisdom. In regard to the location of Sheba in Africa has more grounding, I see this woman as an African. What the Queen had in her country could be compared with the king for the purpose of certifying that the latter is "able".

Black people go all the way back to the beginning of time. Adam and Eve were made out of the dirt of the earth and water. Most Black people have been duped into running from the Bible thinking it was the white man's book and during that time race was not the social and political issue that it is today. Most biblical activity took place in areas historically populated by people of color, such as the Middle East and Northeast Africa. Black ancestry and features are characteristics of Black people. The majority of people referred to in the Bible would have to be classified as Black

Black preachers, scholars and historians are determined to shed more light on the presence of Black kings, queens and war leaders and women of the Bible. They say that the Biblical hermeneutics tells us that African American people identified with their in heritage. African people were very much embedded in the founding of the Judeo-Christian religion.

The biblical book Zephaniah, he was a Black Man called the "son of Cush". Zephaniah was counted among the minor prophets of the Bible. Some people read King Solomon's lyrical prose in the Sons of Solomon and conclude him to as a Black man and this song like book was devoted to his relationship with the Queen of Sheba.

If Solomon, King David's son, was Black, I think Jesus Christ himself was also, according to the genealogy outlined in the first chapter of Matthew.

Churches like St. Sabina, a Catholic Church in Chicago, and Mores Chapel A.ME. Church in St. Petersburg, Florida have changed their windows and wall paintings that depict biblical characters of whites and soon the Abyssinian Baptist Church of Harlem will do the same. We will see more Black images that are correct.

"Whites in the Bible are Greeks and Romans, Asian are mentioned and so is Hispania". There is a rich Mosaic of diverse people in the Bible that makes it very compelling (Jones 1994).

THE OLD TESAMENT

In the Old Testament, Ethiopia is spoken of with great respect and not the country as a whole.

Genesis 1:26	God created man in his own Image male and female, he created them.
Hagar,	Sarah's Egyptian handmaid.
Exodus 2:21	Moses married an Ethiopian wife, Zipporah.
Genesis 10:7,28	Sheba was a male.
2 Samuel 18:21	A Cushite was used as a messenger.
Job 28:19	A rich land, Ethiopia.
Isaiah 20:3	Jehovah is interested in the children of Ethiopia and history.
40:41	Cush and Mizraub are correctly mentioned as a political unit.
45:16	Ethiopia was engaged in trade with Arabia.
Jeremiah 38:7	Ebed-Mel was Jeremiah's helper.
Ezekial 20:10	A great land and civilized people.
38:5	Ethiopians are warlike.
Nahum 3:9	Ethiopians gave strength to Nineveh.
Psalm 87:4	Ethiopians citizens were proud of their Land.
Amos 9:7	Spoke of the Ethiopians as beings equal to the Israelites in the sight of God probably did so in spite of the fact that the people of his time despised them as a race of slaves. On the other hand, there were periods of Ethiopian rule over Egypt. In the reign of Asa, there was an invasion by "Zerah, the Ethiopian" who is

identified with Osork II (about 900B.C.). The invaders were defeated and driven out.

2 Chronicles 14:9 Mentions Ethiopia Kings by name (Zerah)

2 Kings 17:4 King of Assyria found conspiracy in Rosha and locked up the messenger.

2 Kings 19:9 Tirhakah was a king of Ethiopia; he wanted to make war with Hezekiah (Zondervan 1997).

GIFTS FROM FOREIGNERS

PURPLE DYE—It was a prize color of the Israelites as it was of the Canaanites before them. The dye, which was valued throughout the world, was extracted from the Murex shellfish (a snail) and manufactured in various shades. Solomon sent to Tyree for men skilled in making of purple fabrics (2 Chronicles 2:7).

POLYGAMY—Solomon married to seal political alliances and gained political advantages. The practice or more than one wife appeared to be widely accepted in the Old Testament Times (1 Kings 11:1-3).

HORSES—There were many reasons to raise horses, but a few of them were agriculturally related. Most of the horses were used for military purposes. Consequently the King and the State owned most horses. The Egyptians owned horses but Israel was shunning of them. The major fear of horses was that they would lead a king to love pleasure, leisure, and war (Deuteronomy 17:16).

(1 Samuel 8:11) Solomon was impressed by horse statues and stocked his army with at least 40,000 horses. He paid $150 shekels to have them imported from Egypt. At one point in Israel history, statues of horses (or possible real horses) were in the temple as part of the sun god. 1 Kings 10:26 says that when Solomon did his inventory he found that he had 1,400 chariots, and 12,000 horsemen, whom he bestowed in the cities for wartime, and with the King in Jerusalem (Coleman 1984).

GIFTS TO KING SOLOMON AND CONVERSATIONS

1 Kings 3:4 tells of King Solomon's vision at Gibeon—to upgrade his style, to orient Monarch and to build a new palace, because that being of his father was inadequate. He uplifted Israel to be a world power. Fit almost to rant beside Assyria and Egypt. The credit was due to the vision. He attained a collection of armor; much of it was made of gold and intended for show, not use.

Gifts were calendars, copper tools, fine statues, linen cloth, pottery, perfume, jewels, gems, furniture, leather, spices, silks, precious stones, sorghum, ivory, ostrich feathers, animals male and female, cattle of many kinds, birds (peacocks), mules, corn, sugar cane, dates, bananas, seeds, rice, salt, cotton, iron, bronze, lead, granite, diamonds, silver, salty wood, marble stones, dung cakes, black resin and building stones, incense, and $120 talents of gold (1 Kings 9:26 ff; 10:22). Original spices the Israelites had never seen or smelled:

1. Frankincense—to offer to Solon's God, funeral pyres, antidote for poison, chest pains, hemorrhoids, and paralysis.

2. Myrrh—for preparation of bodies for funerals, healing eyes ears, ailments and for inducing menstrual cycles (Miller 1999).

The Chronicles retained from any criticism of Solomon's reign (I Kings 12th chapter). A man is led by the beauty of God's creation to worship the natural phenomena; humanity subsequently assumes that it can fabricate God and begun to trust in the works of his hands.

The ultimate irony is that Egyptians, who had imprisoned the people of God, are really themselves captive of the power of darkness. Philo Flaccus 162-80 B.C. said the radical drams of the transformation of nature, so that Ur burns in water and yet has no power over human flesh.

The Wisdom of Solomon addressed alien kings in order to teach them how to rule wisely, its purpose in facing persecution and the dangers of idolatry in a pagan culture (Simons 1960).

SHEBA AND SOLOMON'S CONVERSATIONS

From research, the Queen of Sheba (Medeka) was about 24 years old and held her head high. She was tall with a dark olive complexion resembling Grace Jones. She also had a full head of Cole black straight hair, always in royal attire with jewels. There isn't any information on her father as such, only a Cushite mother, Sami, with a bloodline from Noah, Ham, Cush and Nimrod (from Arabia and Ethiopia).

In Sheba the days and nights were equal with its smell of love. Its wide expansion of love was law; it was more powerful than any man, because of the intense heated soft robes men and women wore.

Her education called for reading of reeds and papyrus rolls in urns, animals, and goat skins, on wood, clay paintings and stone carvings that went back nine or ten millennia. The library was housed on a smallish antler (shelf). She was well schooled in disguising, curiosity, restlessness, contempt, and impatience. She knew a lot of mischief. Just by her appearance she startled anyone that ever saw her. Madeka was just pretty with black hair. To this woman she addressed herself, "Who is this man Solomon?" She appreciated everything that ever was or ever would be, like name, marks and symbols.

Madeka was born in Ophir and raised among the women in the Sleeping Gardens of Ethiopia. Se read many books Solomon and Moses wrote.

Since the Sabaeans believed in the moon and sun god, each time it appeared the women bled and when the moon was full again. The women knew they were fertile and conceived. Twelve groups of children were born each year, and the children were happy. Huts and tents were their homes, made of Baobab, and mahogany.

It was good that a man and woman lived together, which was one of the traditions of that day. The sun god was the biggest yellow ball, which brought warmth and light.

In 8 B. C., the Sabeans had established a kingdom of their own with Marib as its capital. The throne was built on wealth. Solomon emperors in Ethiopia are still alive today. In 1955, Haile Selassie was found to have been a descendant of these two personages, reggae music and herbs.

Tamrin, a fleet master (merchant seaman), told Madeka of the palace people, asking for gold, ivory, frankincense, and blue sapphires to be used in a major building project in Jerusalem and offering to pay double than their worth. Solomon was building a tabernacle to offer praises to the Father, and willing to exchange goods for what he needed to build the temple. The Queen's harem had many false windows, a few gazes out into the open sky. Eludy women kept themselves covered. Solomon was building calendars. The Queen laughed at his message. After listening to various stories from Tamrin, she thought of Solomon as being a magician. Her librarian (the Pythoness) was consulted on this matter, telling Madeka that King Solomon didn't use chariots, trade routes and trickery. The greatest thing that was in the country of Solomon was no imperfection.

Solomon gave gold and silver to the merchants and their leaders. When Tamrin heard of this, he went to see him during his trip to Jerusalem. He was told by Solomon to bring whatever he wished from his hometown in Arabia, but he was in desperate need of red wood, gold, black wood that could not be eaten by worms and sapphires that burned like the fires of heaven. So Tamrin saw that Solomon was not just a king, but also a great statesman, moreover, he noticed that the Father had provided him abundance, so that gold was as common as lead, and that each was plentiful as the grass of the fields. So Tamrin, the merchant left the court of Judea and Jerusalem and returned to Ethiopia to meet the Queen, 2,000 miles away to tell her what he had heard and seen. He told her that there were the people that lived under Solomon's rule saying how no man stole from his neighbor, and how there were neither any robbers among them, but the people lived in peace.

Now every morning the Queen asked Tamrin again what he might recall of Solomon and his Kingdom, for she wanted very much to see all of this for herself someday. Like most kings and queens, she sent many nice gifts of gratitude.

The temple was being built on Mount Mariah, with walls of marble stone, the roof of cedar wood. God said to King David, "You have been a man of war and have fought many battles and shed much blood. My house shall be built by a man of peace." For the buildings of the temple, the cedar was brought from Mount Lebanon, where they were cut down and carried to Tyre on the seacoast. There they were made into rafts in the great sea and were floated down to Joppa. At Joppa they were carried ashore and were carried to Jerusalem. All this work was done by the men of Tyre, at the command of their King Hiram, who was a friend of Solomon, as he had been a friend of King David. It took seven years to built a temple. Solomon was crowned by the guards and nobles and anointed by Zadak the priest in Gihon, south of the city, and there were sacrifices and prayers that were answered.

In the meantime, Solomon knew about Queen Medeka's reputation as being on the most wonderful human being on the planet. While sitting in the garden looking up at the sky, Medeka penetrated his inner thought; his ambassadors said she was pretty, the Jewish people that migrated to Ethiopia said he was gorgeous, and even Tamrin said she was also. Visiting her he would have opened the door for silly thoughts, silly games, and stupidity. Those things, he was about to show her, since he had a Kingship (the dark side). Why not personally visit her—no, that would have imposed him. From the Jewish traditions he couldn't have done either of the above, by being the King, he should have been able to add all the nearby or far away provinces women to his Harem.

With Jerusalem being 2,000 miles away from Sheba, Solomon sent Medeka a letter asking her to visit him; in the form of a picture from the flowers enclosed with his seal. He got tires of receiving gifts from her. He said:

"I Solomon, King of Israel, bid thee O' Ancient King saying hasten forthwith and come to me. Your God has equipped you with money and gifts. But come to see a man that's been equipped with light and guidance."

This invitation to Medeka was not for a great dinner telling story to the Israelites of her country and resources. The Jews said if Solomon marries a dark woman it would have been to keep high himself and the nation. She is a woman with a wholesome intelligence.

The librarian interpreted the letter as being a formal invitation to be grateful to Medeka. Gossip and rumors took to the wind. Lust set in the Queen's mind, being a virgin. She longed to watch the truth from his lips of the wisest man on earth. She consented to visit Solomon after listening to four more of Tamrin's stories. She thought of King Solomon's wisdom and wearing apparel, comparing fashions to the women of the North. She wore costumes throughout her empire with precious coal dusk and gems. She was always drawn to new power.

Her treasure contained vats of gold dusk, pots of emeralds, urns of sapphires, blue and red, and a chest of pearls.

Tamrin and Bashir maneuvered her preparation for the journey. Medeka's heart was inclined to go, and thus did the Father put the longing there. So she prepared for a long journey because as she spoke of it to her people, "I am smitten with the love of wisdom," a 2,000 mile journey

As the Queen spoke of the power of wisdom, her people paid heed to what she said, for she explained wisdom was better than the treasure of silver and gold. It is sweeter than honey and finer than wine, brighter than the sun (and yet the sun was her God). To be loved is more than precious stones. What is stored within it is greater than oil, and satisfies one's craving more than meals. It is joy to the heart, light to the eye, speed to the food, and shield to the breast. Wisdom is the best of all treasures. He who stores gold has no profit without wisdom, and he who stores wisdom no one can steal. I believe Queen Medeka of Sheba was a match for King Solomon.

In the book of (Deuteronomy 7:1-3) says Solomon disobeyed several provisions. He multiplies to himself wives, horses, a mass of gold, and that he therein sinned. But an agnostic viewpoint holds that the book was written for the expressing a Solomonic cult (a Jewish twenty-second amendment).

Medeka knew she had to travel by sea and land, so she prepared for it. One month's journey, fighting the wind with care would be her number one problem. Her traveling unit (or train) consisted of 197 camels, mules and asses. She set out on her journey according to a road map and the Father gave her heart.

With King Solomon having several wives and the Bible spoke of his Egyptian wife (Lady Tanis) and later a multitude of them. One would wonder how he was able to keep them in tact, and submissive. The princess of Egypt went to take a Napp. She chose to be absent from the day's festival. She complained of a migraine headache, pretending (denying the reality of the visit of the Queen of Sheba) and she came out later and discussed her belief to the entire kingdom (Levine 1980).

Madeka arrived, much to her dismay, looking at all the Egyptian sphinxes she knew the Egyptians had a foothold in Jerusalem and assumed Solomon had a lot from his Egyptian wife, but in her mind was the entire picture and believed she would become the greatest one and she did. In her mind she shot for the top position in Solomon's mind.

Madeka was rushed to the priestly hut. Solomon with his petty style is vaunted as nobler, loftier, more relevant. I am sure there were many arguments that followed.

After King Solomon accepted her gifts of plenty that exceeded him far above all kingdoms at the same time that he needed them and the land from whence they did come. Multiplication is always at hand (Deen 1955)

Solomon was surprised of the beauty and love that she showed. She was tall and strong. She was wondering of the popular opinion as a guide, mediation or a control. Solomon fell the moment he laid his eyes on her. Secrets started to shadow his window and at the same time, she dealt with the amulet, which she held. Madeka housed a map, a foolish soul, and yet she wrote a beautiful one around her neck.

Sami, Queen Madeka's mother, was back at home in her palace holing her silence periods and ordered complete silence; two-thirds of the six-month period her daughter would be gone to visit King Solomon She herself was a soothsayer. Her prediction for her daughter was to rule, command an army, retain slaves, and have servants; all Sami's predictions came to pass (Ormone 1913).

Directly after the Queen's arrival in Jerusalem, Solomon gave her a place to stay in the royal palace near him. He sent food to her every morning, noon, and night. Gazelles and feathered fowls and measures of old wine (and she was not a wine drinker). He sent her singing men and fine honey, and rich sweets. Every day he arrayed her in garments that bewitched the eyes. And all this was going on while he was building the temple (House of the Father). Everything was wrought by his order and there was no opposition of his word, for the light of his heart was like a lamp in darkness and his words of wisdom were as abundant as the sand grains of the desert. And the speeches of beasts and birds were not hidden from him and he did everything by means of a skill, which the Father had given him. He did not ask for victory over his enemy, or for riches or fame. Solomon only asked for wisdom and knowledge, whereby he might rule his people and build his Father's House.

And the Queen Madeka spoke to King Solomon: I looked upon you and see that your wisdom is immeasurable and your understanding is inexhaustible. These are like pomegranates in the garden, a pearl in the sea, and the morning starts at dawn. I give thanks to your King and our Creator, who brought me here so that I might hear your voice in person.

Her questions: "What starts at 5, and goes to 9, becomes 1 and ends at 2?" Solomon answered: "For 5 days the wombs separated until she conceives: then for 9 months, she carries; then the one inside her is born and cries for 2 breasts.

The Queen told Solomon that they worship the sun, for he cooks their food. And moreover, he illuminates the darkness, removes fear. They called him "their King and Creator". Solomon told her the week comes the moon and she could take it for what it is worth. It is a resting place of all dead matter on earth; it is the mother of tides and lust. She told him she worshiped the sun, not the moon. As she spoke of her family and fertile land, Solomon listened and then retired for the night in separate quarters.

Some thought they would marry and some thought to be alive on this day was a disgrace. The second time she appeared she bowed to King Solomon; the most important thing was that she was there during the temple construction to God. She thought most Gods were good for the world, and she saw them as so many lovers, and they hungered for a higher change than her own. An untangle movement, progress and the revolution that they suggested. But her hope that they would be good lovers to her and her people was fearful. Her princes and advisors had told her to reserve judgment. She at this point had begun to build her trust in him admiring his uniqueness.

Bathsheba, Solomon's mother, feeds Solomon with lotus and cottonseed to make him sterile because she did not like the Egyptian wife. The Egyptian women had a history of being fast and acting like a throne. But what Bathsheba forgot was when Solomon fasted and sacrificed her burdens fell to his feet. Tales of the strong lover that was sent to the bath house three times each time they made love, because there was where they met.

Solomon discusses his family members with her and tells of how refreshing it is to be in her presence and at the same time testing her to see if she is guided by the truth and guidance. And they both retired for the night.

The second month they toured the entire palace, prepared for a small festival lunch and at the change of the guard, the attending servants in their robes, his valers and the burnt offering he made in the temple of the Lord. Solomon told Madeka each time she was to appear a great crowd would come, "You don't change a whit about you, you are every bit a nice looking in the morning as you are in the afternoon." She had the appetite of 10 men.

Solomon had a library in the palace as well as Sheba. He even had information on Ethiopia and Egypt. The library was overflowed with records to be sorted and written down in their proper place and time, a wilderness of dates and place to be classified for the first time since the exodus from Egypt, close to 500 years ago. The parade was of musicians, dances and tambourines in the Palace.

When the Queen first heard of the fame of King Solomon (due in the name of the Lord), she gathered all the hard questions to ask him.

Because of the Lord's "Eternal love for Israel, he made you King to maintain justice and righteousness." King Solomon gave to her all she asked for, for the time being. Not it was time match her intelligence with the present wife and found that she was just as smart, or smarter. Solomon, Madeka thought has the knowledge in her veins to believe she would end up an Egyptian bride. She could take up the boy-man idea with an authority that her mother did not have, nor the Egyptian warriors and their conquered wives and concubines. They are in the gardens she is reassuring and sampling, and embracing him. Trying her I would call it.

Solomon answered Queen Madela's wisdom and understanding sprang from her heart too. As for me, I have them only because I asked him (the father of Israel) and he gave them to me. I do not serve according to the fathers. My speech springs not from myself but it only is what the father makes me utter. Whatsoever he commands me to do, I say whatever he teaches me to speak. For once I was dust and now I am flesh, once I was water and now I am solid, for the father fashioned me in his own likeness and made me in his own image (Zodervan 1997).

Questions to be answered on politics, of sex and of science, tide phrases, water churning sounds, like in the core of women and does provide him and he only wants to prong and slay. She felt him a worthy adversary and something will happen between then and she was willing to risk it; he knew all that was hidden and did not hid anything from her, that why she paid attention to him.

Jerusalem was about to be enjoyed. Gray buildings of the city City out showed all others. The wall had many open door assesses. The Queen took this for a sign that the King of Israel was concerned with protocol and legitimacy. Each entrance led to a passage guard. Even the paying station was pretty; arena personnel were paid $17,000 in gold. Madeka and Solomon sat in the gardens and they ate whatever they were served.

Questions arose again and again and believe me; King Solomon was ready to answer them:

1. Who is the devil?
    a. A cute thing, like a pet animal—wrong thoughts and the Lord monitors
    good and evil and in them is the definition,
2. Are eyes or ears superior?
    a. Degree of deafness and blindness, they are man's provinces and measurable.
3. What is the most important organ in the body?
    a. Death and life are in the power of the tongue.
4. How are the body and spirit connected?
    a. The baseness of the spirits is derived from the bodies, and the bodies from
    the spirits.
5. How do you dare challenge the absolute continuity of mother and daughter or how can an economic system based on paternity can be reliable?
    a. Solomon relied there is scientific accuracy in motherhood.
    b. The blood of a child is magnetic to the bone of the mother and father
    living or dead.
6. What do you know about Moses?
    a. Solomon answered, "He married a Shebian, Zipporah, and Moses married
    twice.

7. What is the different between male and female?

    a. Solomon said, by throwing objects to both, the girls will choose to close their legs and the boys will open theirs.

    b. If you pour water into both right hands, the girls will moisten their faces and the boys will pour water into the one and throw it down.

    c. The sexless one was called in to help the king; they were technicians of the male dominated society.

8. What is the disposition of the people?

    a. The Jews use disposition of clothing, the Arabs discuss male verses female, modes of washing, the Ethiopians stimulate that meals contain meat, bread, and beer. The females prefer fruit and sweets.

Madeka returned to the hall of justice in Solomon's palace to enjoy a checker game and later to her quarters for the night. Her bed had a star canopy, a thousand instruments on the printed sheets, with its own god. They were made of gold and silver threads and played by women. The Talmud said next on Solomon's list was to personally introduce her to laborers in the work place. He stopped one worker that had his protect gear and skin of water to shell out his thoughts about his economical living conditions. Solomon hailed him to half and the laborer stood still.

Then the king turned to the queen and said, "Look at this man. Am I superior to him? I am a man of dust and ash who will soon become worms and yet at this moment I appear like one who will never die. Both of us are beings, that is to say, men. His death is my death; his life is my life is my life. This man is stronger as a worker than I am, for the Father has given power to show as it pleases him to do." Then Solomon released the laborer.

Solomon then said to the queen, "Of what use are we the children of men, if we do not use kindness and love? Are we not grass upon the field, which withers in its season and is burnt by fire? We wear clothes and eat excellent food and we bathe ourselves in sweet scent, and yet being wise we are fools. The man made in the image of the father should be like him. Let the arrogant and the honor less be judged along with the David structure. For the Father loves the humble and those who practice humility, walk in the way of the father and rejoice in his kingdom. Blessed is the man who knows wisdom, which is to say compassion, which is to say the love of the father.

Then the Queen said to the Solomon, "How greatly your words please me." Tell me now whom shall I worship; we worship the sun because he cooks our food and he lightens the darkness. We call him our king, our creator; we worship him as a God, for no man has told us that there is another. But now we hear there is one that is with you in Israel, another God, whom we do not know. Men have told us that he sent you a tabernacle and a tablet, ordered by angels and delivered by the hand of Moses. This we have heard and that he, himself, has come down to you and has talked to you giving you his commandments.

Solomon said, "Is it right that man should worship the Father, for he created the Universe, heaven and earth; he created the sea and dry land, the sun and the moon and the stars; he made the trees and the stones, the beasts and the fowls, the crocodiles and the fish; he made the whales and the hippopotamus, the water lizards and the gazelles; therefore, it is right that we should worship him with gladness for the father is the Lord of the Universe, the maker of angels and me; it is he who punishes and he shows compassion; it is he who exalts and he who condemns, is it he who raised up and he who brings down and who among us can say to him what have you done?"

And Queen Madeka said, "From this time forward I shall no linger worship the sun, but I shall worship the creator of the sun, the God of Israel." And so it was that the queen went to Solomon and he answered the questions, which she put to him. But after she had dwelt there 5 months the queen wished to return to her own country, so she sent a message to Solomon: "I greatly wish to remain here with you, but now, for the sake of my own people, I must return to my country, as for that which I have heard let the Father make bear fruit in my heart and in the hearts of all those who will hear it from me."

And King Solomon in return sent a message to the Queen: "Will you go away without seeing the entire kingdom and without dinning with me?" And the queen replied, "From being a fool I have become wise listening to your wisdom. Therefore, I shall stay according to your desire." Then Solomon had his palace and the royal table set according to the law of his kingdom. The queen came and she was struck with wonder of the splendor of that which she had seen These were purple hangings and carpets, marble and precious stones and incense that burned, aromatic powder and the scent of myrrh, cassis, and frankincense came from all directions.

And Solomon sent meals to her chamber, which would make her thirsty, and drinks mingled with vinegar and other dishes spiced with pepper. She had an appetite of 10 men. After the meal, the king rose up and went to the queen and they were alone together. He said to her, "Take your ease here for ones' sake until daybreak." She said to him, "Swear to the God of Israel that you will not take me by force." Solomon answered, "I swear that I will not, but you will not take by force any of my possessions." Solomon gave to her old wine from old kegs, and she did not drink. H sent dancers to entertain her (Ormode 1954).

The Queen laughed at hearing this and replied, "I have no need of your things as you know I am wealthy. Nevertheless I swear that I will not take any of your possessions" and he swore to her and made her swore to him. The king went up on his bed on one side of the chamber. Servants made ready her bed on the opposite side. And Solomon said to a young manservant, "Wash out the bowl, and set in it a vessel of water while the queen is looking on, then shut the doors and leave us in peace."

After answering most of her questions, she found Solomon irresistible depending more on him. Solomon would have valued her and at the same time think little of all women. Will she reform him, save him or dump him. Madeka was left-handed.

Solomon asked Madeka would she steal his heart from out of his left side and put it in a mirror, only to make him mad? "David felt at the end he would have to escape his own sword." Those who strive to confute our revelation shall suffer the torment of a harrowing scourge.

Madeka found that truth and love would be indistinguishable for her and wisdom and science were for others.

Now the king pretended to be asleep, being he was really watching the queen. For her part, she slept for a while and then awoke, with her throat dry with thirst, for the food had made he thirsty. Now she looked up at King Solomon and watched him carefully. At last she decided he was asleep, but he was not asleep, he was waiting until she should rise up to steal the water that was put between

So the queen rose up and went to the water in the bowl and lifted the jar to drink. Solomon seized her hand before she could drink and said, "Why have you broken your oath that you would not take by force anything in my house." Was the oath broken by drinking the water? "Then I have sinned against myself and you are free of your oath," she told him, "I am free from the oath which you made me swear."

"Yes you are pleased, let me drink your water." Solomon permitted her to drink and he found Medaka a virgin and a pretty Black woman. Solomon drew near to her as she drank her last drink; he stood over her bed with bid walf-teeth gleaming at her. "I want you for your lonely body, for your even temple, and for your marvelousness, an escape route was out of the question for her. He ran his fingers through her black hair and leaned backward on his bed. He found she was innocent of both reflection and freedom. He kissed her before she could say a word or do anything else. She knew it from the very moment, he tasted good, so warm, so tasty. When his mouth moved on and teeth nibbled at her ear lobes, she managed to perform a protest. "What are you doing?" Madeka asked. She squirmed because she was a virgin; she submitted herself, her spirit that is, but she tried to stealthily away from him but almost cut off from him. He turned unexpectedly on her and anchored her in position, and the satin gown disappeared. His eyes met hers and the long moment went by dealing with a 200-pound man. Every nerve in her body was attuned to the invasion, wanting more, groping blindly; she clouded her eyes. Hands founds her every body part to make sure there wasn't one missing. Madeka's mind slipped completely out of control. "Oh, Jehovah," she moaned. She suddenly became cold and hot at the same time. Her body jerked a few times, looking for its wonderful tormentor who was no longer there. She knew with a sudden eagerness fired from his eagerness that was a hard, rough, and good situation that was to be enjoyable, making the way to become his wife. She opened one eye, only to see Solomon sitting on the edge of the bed rubbing himself.

Of course, after the first encounter Madeka wanted to penetrate Solomon's thoughts. He told her, he had never met a woman that he was turned on so quickly and didn't want to let go so thoroughly made.

"Nonsense, you believe it comes with the territories or practices."

"Who me? Not a chance." In his mind having sex with a virgin, having to regroup, he lost his body spirit many times with this woman, but never before. Solomon thought he would lay in and relax for a while telling Madeka parables, war stories, about other men vanity stories, and foretold her future.

Now she must tell him her thoughts hoping not to disappoint him. He told him. She told him she was completely satisfied, having the best of everything. He told her there was no need to go through life suffering for something, which he could provide so easy. You hear me, Madeka! She told him she heard him very faintly under her breath. All her hatreds and inhibitions had disappeared at that moment. All the joys that had been suppressed for a while came back into her flower.

Solomon asked Madeka to marry him. A marriage was between the two of them. Evidently Madeka had this planned bringing the ring for King Solomon with her. After she offered the ring, "the Spirit went out of her and returned".

Solomon's special pet, the Whoopee bird, was mad because he could not hear the conversation. Both Bath-Sheba and Queen Madeka were well liked by him. If a census had been taken been taken at the kennel he would have been missing (Badge 1922).

There was never a king like Solomon
not since the world began,
yet Solomon talked to a butterfly
as a man would talk to a man.
By Rudyard Kipling

As the scripture tells us, the wise King Solomon, the son of King David "spake also of beasts and fowls, of creeping things, and of fish. The oldest biological lecture, has given rise to the charming legend that the king was able to talk the language of animals, which was hidden from all other man." I believe Solomon really could do so. Even without the magic ring, which the credit is given to it. He could without the aid of magic, black, white, or otherwise, without supernatural assistance, our fellow creatures can tell us the most beautiful stories.

Can the "the signal code" be called a language? Believe or not man had a hidden vocabulary. A baby or kid certainly knows a lot of psychology, why, how, and where and when to apply it. And if a parent isn't careful the child will win.

By listening to the vocabulary of some highly social species of beast or bird it is often possible to attain to an astonishing intimacy and mutual understanding. To scientific investigating animal behaviors this becomes a matter of course and ceases to be source or wonder.

Animals can be nuisances, especially the lazy ones. If you feed one on a daily basis, he will continue to return to your palace (the dog) at the same time. He will make no effort to clean up after himself, like we are taught. One after the other will clean, and give now medical care.

There is always robbery in an aquarium. Let us know that the largest fish will eat the small ones, and it becomes the survival of the fittest, unless the groups are mismatched. Fish is always exposed to light and people; they need oxygen and give off carbon dioxide like we do. And certainly nothing and nobody can live without food.

Why do we stand and laugh at the monkeys and at the same time we are afraid of insects (caterpillars); it is evolutionary adaptation. We think an animal that is near or next to our species doing several tricks then it becomes funny. The public us then dividing things which to me, are holy: The riddles of the Genesis, the creation and the creator, the forms of chameleons, ants birds, ducks, rats, goats, etc. The cast would have been 100%.

After two strong ordeals, Solomon felt sleepy and weak. As he slept, a vision appeared to him. He saw a brilliant sun come down from heaven and shred great splendor Israel. There it remained for a while, but suddenly withdrew itself and flew away to the country of Ethiopia, where shone brightly forever. Solomon waited to see if the brilliancy would come back to Israel; it did not return. Then, while he waited, a light rose up in the heaven and another sun came down in the country of Judah, and it sent forth light, which was stronger than before.

Now Israel, because of the flame of the sun, refused to walk in the light itself. And the sun paid no heed to Israel and the Israelites hated him and became impossible that peace should exist between them and the sun, and they rose to extinguish that sun. Thus they cast darkness upon the while wide world. Earthquakes came, followed by thick darkness. They had destroyed his light and put a guard over his tomb. His tomb wherein they casted for him, and illumined the whole world. Those places most bathed in his light were the first sea, the last sea, Ethiopia, and Tome. And he paid no attention whatsoever to Israel and he ascended his former throne.

When Solomon, the king saw this vision he became disturbed. His understanding went away and he worked with a troubled mind; he was actually looking at the future.

After sex King Solomon and Madeka lusted for each other, making sure one would not long for the other. Torn between two poles, Makeda came toward the end of a 6-month stay in Israel. Abandoning her country would be an act of treason, which was a provision of the law, but not prevail. Now the two of them with intermingled thoughts, she said to him that his love will be divided and many times afterward. He often thought about her and her virginity and he told her of the gift that comes with the women, and at that point only Egyptian women.

The Queen said to Solomon, "Let me depart to my own country." Solomon gave her camels and wages and had them laden with the beautiful things. He gave her a vessel whenever one could traverse the wing. These Solomon made by the wisdom, which God had given to him. Wait I have more to tell you. We buy animals according to our needs and wants. When picking your animal you might need help. One has to consider the time, patience and space. Checking the vocabulary is very important before beginning to train. Animal dealers and veterinarians have to be checked because you have to bond with nature. Read lots of books on your animals or pets.

The language of animals is very unique. In a sense, to us they do because I have been around many animals, when one of his own species gave an order or asked a question, the others adhered to it. Humans behave in a like manner; no one knows when the other is tired, and he will retire. Some animals and birds imitate humans (parrots and dogs). All animals have memory, so be direct in what you train them for.

Roah, the raven, and King Solomon's pet that accompanied him everywhere, he spoke to Solomon in human words, but to his kind he used to call notes. He brightens strangers and foreign places. He also ran a check and balance system for the king to test him of moments and directions. Solomon was not the only man that could talk to the animals.

The covenant with an animal is an example (the bond of a man and his dog). The dog was the first domestic animal to become man's friend. The thought if the covenant was signed since the dog has always followed man from day one. He is easy to train, to be a protector of your domain as well as carrying heavy loads. And he considers man as his master and not the lead dog. They are faithful and respectful. It doesn't take but a few day to make the bond.

A dog will parade in a soldierly manner to and fro, like a sentinel on guard. When food is left out, he will eat it, and his stomach never fills. Name changing is easy if you feed him (Lonenz 1976).

Solomon answered all of her questions; her curiosity was in no way disappointed. The actual Wisdom of Solomon fully matched his pre-established reputation. The Sabean people over which the Queen ruled were always governed by priestly kings (Psalm 72:12). No doubt the queen took back to her native land glowing reports from Tamrin (her seaman) and other ambassadors were greatly exaggerated. Now she admitted, "the half had never been told to her". Her astonishment arose, not only from what she had been assured, but a triumphant trip to commune with him. The king welcomed him constantly with honor, granting her full rights to survey his riches. But the queen doubted Solomon and began to question herself of his reputation and at the same time felt satisfied.

Ethiopia and the Land of Madeka were under one monarchal rule. This single government was probably constituted in respect of kingship. Both countries were of the same ethnic background, "Ethiopians". During the scattering of Babel, some of Ham's children journeyed north and south of Arabia; three of them were Ramah, Sheba and Dedan, all descendants of Cush (Genesis 10:7, II Chronicles 21:16). It was Madeka who populated the Southern Peninsula and later built the wealthy country called "Sheba" (Isaiah 60:6; Ezekiel; 27:2-23), which remained popular during Solomon's empire.

Madeka's mother, Ekeye spent lots of time in Africa by an Arabian writer (Hamani) who lived in the 10th century. Whenever Madeka needed advice from wise men she sent to the land of Solomon and Hiram of Tyree.

The earliest temple was at Marib, the capital of Sheba, called Mahram Bilguis precincts of the Nikaulis, Queen of Ethiopia and Egypt.

Second, an Austere Rock Pavilion was built so she could not go there to mope, thinking of Solomon for she would not give up their homes, even for their marriage. It is similar to the temple in Jerusalem; there she heard his voice. There were always cultures created in his stories.

While she was married to King Solomon, Madeka laid in darkness, hearing Solomon's loose steps in the night. What she discovered, she heard food steps in her heart. The door was opening and "all the men were coming to her bed. King Solomon's voice said he loved her as well."

Madeka, the Queen of Sheba, found Solomon to have been the wisest one, the all-knowing one, and merciful and said, "Blessed be the name of Jehovah", Solomon's God. Solomon being the man he was and his tradition he remarried 40 days after Madeka's return to Egypt and Ethiopia carrying his child. Madeka did not remarry until after King Solomon's death and Menelik, her only child, Solomon's son, was 30 years old and she was 54 when she married one of her top generals (Levine 1980).

WORDS TO THE QUEEN

I am smitten with the love of wisdom, and I am constrained by the cords of understanding for wisdom is far better than treasures of gold and silver, and wisdom is the best of everything that has been created on the earth. It is sweeter than honey, and it is to be loved more than precious stones. Wisdom is an exalted thing and a right thing; I will love her like a mother, and she will embrace me like I am her child.

Through wisdom I have dived down into the great sea, and have seized in the place of her depth like a pearl, whereby I am rich. I went down like the great iron anchor whereby men anchor ships for the night on the high seas, and I received a lamp which lighten me, and I stood up by the ropes of the boat of understanding, I went to sleep in the depths of the sea, not being overwhelmed with the water. I dreamed a dream, and it seemed a marveled threat, and I lay upon it and made it strong in the splendor of the sun. I went in through the doors of the treasury of wisdom and I drew for myself the waters that were standing. I went into the blaze of the flame of the sun, and it lighted me with the splendor there of, and I made a shield for myself, and I saved myself by confidence therein and not myself only for those that travel in the footprints of wisdom, and not myself only but not only those who travel in their ways the nations that are round about (Busby 1994). *Copy editor here! Is the highlighted passage a direct quotation from an outside source? If so, we have to put it in quotation marks. Thanks!*

HOW ETHIOPIA POLITICALLY GAINED FROM HER VISIT

With the respect to the Queen of Sheba, she has been regarded over the extent that she was an historical personality. She was the ruler of the Sabean people in the Southwestern Arabia and Ethiopia. Interestingly, Josephus saw her as the Queen of Egypt and Ethiopia. Her home was the Arabic Flex, a place of royal sport for rulers throughout the world with a reputation to test each other's abilities, similar to the Olympic in the arena. Its main purpose was to test his wisdom with performance.

Thus the achievements, literature, sciences, their daily life contacts with the world were spread far and wide and the foundations of later civilization. Egypt's early political organization and practical arts became the starting point for others. For this reason Egypt has been called the "Cradle of Civilization".

The queen had the good reason to feel that her diplomatic mission would not be successful. We have to remember that Solomon invited her.

The Queen of Sheba was the first reigning queen on record who pitted her wits and wealth against those of a king. The real purpose of her visit was probably the trade demarcation and alliance she worked out with Solomon. Solomon's commercial expansion flowed as well as hers after her visit. Sabean women occupied positions nine centuries before Jesus Christ. At that time women enjoyed the same civil, religious and even military functions.

For many centuries the Queen of Sheba's visit had been a popular subject for the old masters. She was elegant, dignified, and wore apparel that was neither too costly, nor gaudy. She was depicted as having a girlish figure, entering Solomon's court in great haste and running up the steps of the dais to meet the king. A painting in the Gallery at Sidney, Wales (United Kingdom in Southwestern, Great Britain) portrays the Queen of Sheba as a woman splendidly attire and located with Jews by Sir E J. Poyner showing a wealthy woman (Delitzsch 1680).

Sheba had fame and fortune, very cultural and great political power (Psalm 72:10; Isaiah 60:6; Jeremiah 6:26). The definition of power means "valor," "rue," "strength," "authority," or "right." Power is attributed permanently to God (Chronicles 29:11). The power of God (omnipotence) is the supreme manifestation of the power, as the wisdom and love of God as in redemption (1 Corinthian 1:18-24). Power also means the keys to open doors and after one attains it, it is up to us to keep it balanced because the consequences might result in madness, lust, greed, and hatred which leads to the fall of an empire. The exchange of gifts is one of the first empires. The exchange of gifts is one of the first relations for business purposes on record.

The Queen of Sheba was a wise woman herself and saw in her visit and opportunity for trade between her country or commercial expansion followed even as far as Asia and Asia Minor (Deen 1955).

Whatever the reason for her visit it was a personal triumph for Solomon, for she came bearing splendorous tributes and the King's intellect. The reference to the name of the Lord in an additional Deuteronomistic twist that one does not find in the parallel account in (Chronicles 9:1) which has the Queen's visiting only to authenticate the rumors. In the review, the narrator's point to what is theologically crucial in the entire Lord that's in question (Badge 1922).

The Bible sees Queen Madeka as a rich potentate on an economical mission. The Hebrews thought Madeka was too pushy and too homely for King Solomon to be attractive to her. They did not want Solomon and Madeka together to generate so much power. They favored David to Solomon, and they enjoyed the high lights of the modern circuit and a land of plenty.

Solomon's reign marks the peak of Israelite success both politically and implies that some credit should be made. It was in Solomon's reign that the promises made to the Patriarch (1 Kings 4:20) on the other hand of syncretism and the influx of foreign practices under Solomon mark the beginning of the religious decay, accompanied which had grown internally and the emergence of external enemies.

After Madeka settled down at home immediately after the visit, I believe she did a comparison of the number of provinces, materials population and geographical boundaries, and finding that she was the richest. The Ethiopian dollar was the dollar of that time. Also, whatever King Solomon thought that she needed, he supplied it.

The communiqué of the Queen of Sheba may be just the sort of rhetorical nicely one might expect in a diplomatic mission. Her words were very flattery and fit the Jews' knowledge. Solomon is recognized as a brilliant and glamorous ruler (Langhbaum 1989).

She was one of the rulers far and wide who sought to learn about Solomon's wisdom. Others sent ambassadors. But a courageous and resourceful woman who took an active part in increasing the prosperity of her own people, because of this she was successful.

The Queen of Sheba came to prove lives on now, nearly five centuries since her visit to Israel as a woman whose spirit of any queen in history has not surpassed adventure and certainly her sense of a good public and international relations is unparalleled among the women of the Bible.

After looking at the royal rank, thinking she had more to give, coming from the most resourceful territory, she knew she would have to travel the rank and take her rightful position in history very quickly. When a woman thinks she can out rank possible two or more wives and many after according to the traditions of that day, her thoughts must be strong and not stop at any boundaries. I know a lot of women that are sexy at all, but would enjoy being a member of a Harem because of glamour, no work, plenty of food, and other necessaries and a roof other their heads (Happy).

1 Kings 10:1-3 While archaeologists believe that Solomon may have brought himself into conflict with the Queen of Sheba, one purpose of her famous visit to

Solomon was to establish a trade agreement between Solomon's Kingdom and her own nation (Orr 1915).

Solomon had made the south Arabian Kingdom great; the excuse for her visit, of course, would be her desire to see the famous king. Hard questions probably riddle or test of practical sagacity, wisdom, practical wisdom, and administrative wisdom. The final climax was nearly reached after seeing all of the other splendid things that Madeka had witnessed especially his burnt offerings, which he offered. She was left breathless, and she told Solomon he had added to the wisdom and goodness to the fame she had heard. She saw that all of his wives were happy. Her gifts to him were 120 talents of gold, spices, and other things. His gift to her, according to ancient tradition, the Queen took back with her a child, begotten by Solomon from the Emperor of Ethiopia traces his direct lineage. He just gave in a way commensurate with the resources of such a king (Molyer 1953).

The Queen's visits tighten her political and economical world under her reign.

Solomon said in a vision he chose wisdom rather than wealth and empowered by gifts so that his name became famous throughout the world. His vision brought visitors from all over the world.

Solomon, in his old age, however, fell into sin, sowing seeds of evil, which brought forth a plentiful crop after his death. He reigned for 40 years (II Samuel 22:24) (Sims & Dent).

MENELIK, THE QUEEN'S ONLY SON

An ancient work generated in Ethiopia for centuries about Madeka returning home carrying the child of her union with Solomon.

Tamrin, Madeka's messenger, illuminated her feelings before her journey to Solomon, on hearing of the child, said he loved him and without seeing him and the whole story has been told to me, as the desire of my heart and like water to a thirsty man and afterwards.

Makeda studied Solomon's wisdom and integrity as a ruler and brought it to Ethiopia. When her child began to stir in her body, Solomon's patience and sensitivity were rewarded. She sought advice and help from her closest friends on rearing children and found that there were wives who followed the leads of their husbands. Solomon found Madeka enjoyed sex, but not as he did. Maybe by being pregnant that was the problem, very modest.

Solomon learned her habits and talents. To him she was a historian, and an athlete (once a participator in the Olympics), was very rigid in her pietas deeply believing in her conversion to Jehovah.

Menelik was born with the help of midwives. He weighed in at ten pounds, very healthy, but Madeka was brave. Solomon constantly checked on his latest family periodically. Then having borne Menelik, Madeka intended to be a personal part of a great man forever, King Solomon. Solomon's wisdom was so great that it sped throughout Arabia among those tribes, which were famous. Solomon's periodical visits were to have his son taught the moral principles that he himself ignored all of his life. He had never made a "promise" before. He thought it would help and it might have. What would he give? What if he wanted the child to be his successor (a king), a priest, a judge, or an archive keeper? Well thoughts penetrate men's minds. How can one make the world a better one for his son, maybe to send the Ark of the Covenant into his hometown?

On his first visit he found Menelik asleep with a fat tummy from he mother's milk to bind the child. A long conversation was talked of the upbringing. Solomon tasted the milk for nourishment proteins, and checking Madeka's physical mental health at the same time. Solomon learned that physical love between a mother and her son could be dangerous. So his first visit was complete. The two of them fell asleep and later Solomon said to himself that he was not sorry he bargained with God for them.

Menelik (means son of kings), Ebna Hakin (means son of the wise). He knew his mother's position, having her name on most buildings. He played with most children his own age publicly. His education was somewhat different from prior generations before him. That was done to prime him for her position. Queen Madeka wanted him to be tutored in regular subject matter to bring to Ethiopia the sciences and the wisdom of King Solomon. Madeka did not want her son in the grain fields getting dusty and stinky with the odors of the animals, vegetables, or attending flowers in the rose gardens because one becomes accustomed to lower paying skills he would become complacent.

He was to stay near his mother and her sisters to learn their needs of these following theories:

1. To learn all four corners of the earth,
2. Tutors (all specializers),
3. To learn power and struggle,
4. To be exposed to Leaders and War Warriors,
5. Mountain climbing — Misjudge College

6. Mental Institution;
   a. Women without breast, the frail and jocular,
   b. Defenseless old men telling Old War Stories.

When Menelik was twelve years old, Madeka wanted to introduce him to the dance theater. After looking at dancers perform for eight years. By then he was familiar with most of the body movements. He probably consented to dance training, but ninety percent of his mind was focused on other things.

Madeka noticed Menelik was not be easily satisfied. He was, she thought, the exact image of King Solomon.

Once he focused on his goals, nothing jumped on his train. I believe Solomon visited Ethiopia quite frequently to visit his son, to make sure he was circumcised and to check his manly growing body structure. His visits were secretly planned and accomplished with a short convoy of soldiers. His annual contacts were honored. Madeka was consulted about the training to make sure he had the best of both worlds. Whenever Menelik appeared in any contests in the sports arena, Solomon was there in disguise, cheering his son on toward the finishing line, and having his mother not very far off. Many messengers and writers were there to spread the news. Arena sports were the number one and two priorities of that day because it showed bravery, strength, understanding, direction and guardian care. Shepherds were also there to see just how mean-spirited their animals were.

Sami, Madeka's mother, also imputed many parental ideals as well. She studied the grandson on a daily basis. The tutors were constantly teaching when Madeka was not around, knowing one day he would be a king, sense he was kingly and queenly. His curfew was so in tact to avoid tiredness and weird looks. Menelik's travel orders to socialize with his friends were carefully checked. The nannies were prompted in their understanding and so were the Ministers of Ethiopia.

Menelik did not visit his father until he was a grown youth. Like any young man or woman cannot control the magnetism of the blood. One won't rest until the draw is even. The inkling arose him and permission was granted. A caravan was gathered and travel began. At the age twenty-two Menelik traveled to Jerusalem to visit his father and he said he did not need his mother's marriage ring (wedding ring) for identification. Of all the stories he had heard of his father, wondering and thinking if he were really a look alike. If he were a look a like he would have very little trouble, if any at all. When he arrived in Gaza, the guards and people knew from his appearance that he was King Solomon's son. He was received with honor. A guard approached to the King's chamber telling King Solomon of his son's arrival. Immediately all the schedules stopped. From the top of the stair cage, he recognized his son Menelik. The two walked approaching the bar (middle section between here and there). When Menelik finally reached his father, Solomon stated, "He is still as handsome as ever. He was even handsomer than he ever was and his form and statue were those of King David in his early manhood." Solomon kissed and embraced his son, and immediately received him with high honor.

Solomon highly recognized that Menelik was the first-born; he also plotted to steal the arch of the covenant from the temple of Jerusalem to give to his son. Judaism was a dominant religion in Ethiopia and Christianity later became the dominant one. It was the invention from the time of restoration of the Solomonic Dynasty under the Yekuno Amlak in the thirteenth century. Meantime back home Madeka declared that the fame of Solomon's son wisdom would penetrate through Menelik to her kingdom, and she witted herself to satisfy herself of the truth of the report by personal experience; because Solomon showed to her all of his glory and solved all the riddles which she put to him.

I think Menelik spent at least six months with his father, King Solomon, the same amount of time his mother spent when she visited his father for the first time. There were sites to see and people to get to know, festive activities were scheduled to introduce his son to the world. There were games in the arena to show Menelik the art of man's strength being measured by animals and their shepherds. Sabbath was held to further instill Jewish customs. Mannerism was very much noticed. His wives were Egyptian, Ethiopian, Moabites, Ammonites, Edomities, Zidonians, Hittites, and Phoenicians. All were on the same footing, frolicking in certain places, and entering King Solomon's quarters on request. He was told that there was no jealousy among them. People were in uniforms of color; even the young women were in gay colored flocks. Time was of essence with the king; he liked for his meals to be calorie balanced and on time, consisting of meat and fruit. Menelik loved the chariot declarations and stables. He wanted to spend more time in them, but Solomon told him his hired hands job was to keep them fit and ready upon his request.

After the third month of conversations, King Solomon was equal to find his stand with the young man; the questions Menlik wanted answered were:

1. Father, how does one keep everything and everybody in tack?
    a. I am in charge, the King.
2. How much does it take for upkeep of his place?
    a. Tons of silver, wood, bronze, and stone.
3. Is the income by taxation?
    a. Yes.
4. How many wives do you have?
    a. As many as I can take care of.
5. How many children do you have?
    a. Right now, one and that's you.
6. How many provinces do you own?
    a. All the nearby ones and some day Egypt, Europe, and Asia Minor.

At the end of the fifth month, living there wasn't so bad. But, Father, will you visit us again?

Yes, Menelik. I visited many times to look on you. Each time you grew an inch I was there.

At the end of the sixth month, Solomon asked him to stay. He could not stay because he had promise his mother to return. Solomon had promise Menelik the Kingship of Israel upon his death, but Menelik replied, "My Lord, it is impossible for me to abandon my country and my mother." He swore with his head on his mother's breast that he would return home. That was considered a stone-age bond and it still holds true today, but is seldom used.

When Solomon realized that he could not persuade his don to remain in Jerusalem, he anointed Menelik King of Ethiopia. Bestowed upon him in the name of King David, and provided him with councilors and officers for the founding of Israel's New King of Ethiopia except for a brief period during the ninth and tenth centuries, until the demise of Hail Selassie, Queen Madeka descendants ruled the throne of Ethiopia.

Menelik was set for homecoming with an army of Israelite Warriors and company of priests headed by Ebiathar, who was to teach the Ethiopians the

Jewish faith. The priests however stole the Ark (Tabot, equivalent to Tebah) of the Covenant and the Tablets of the Law and conveyed them to Axum, at the Capital of Ethiopia. This genuine Ark was preserved for many years in the Church at Axum, where Solomon, after a vain attempt to pressure the fugitives, who were protected by the Archangel, was compelled to make copies of the Ark and the Tablets for the temples.

I was told that historical and biblical accounts indicated that the Queen of Sheba was so loved by King Solomon that the Ark was entrusted to her care. And there is an annual display of the Ark, which is held in the month of April, and no one is allowed to touch but the sacred.

Also there is a genetic confirmation that King Solomon had several rendezvous with the Queen of Sheba, but produced only one son. This led to a strong bond between Ethiopian Jews, American Jews, and Israeli Jews.

Menelik first conquered the country and made Judaism its official religion, which it remained until 33 C. E. Then Ethiopia was converted to Christianity, the rulers of Ethiopia bore the title "Loin of Judah " and their official decrees were prefixed by the formal "Loin Of The Judah Hath Triumphed" (badge 1922).

The only evidence remaining of the civilization of Ethiopia are numerous reins of moments and temples on which bottles for religious ceremonies and the industries are represented by sculptures. The first king of Ethiopia was Menelik, son of Madeka. The kings and queens have been found on sculptures on some of the reins. The Ethiopian Language, more correctly called the Geez Language, was introduced from the South Arabian Area and formed the Ancient Ecclesiastical and official language of Abyssinia. Semitic in construction, it resembled Hebrew, Arabic and many others. The modern nomadic tribes of the Sudan and Tyree speak a language quite loosely allied to it.

Madeka told Menelik of her love for his father and his history, and no other nearby man was her equal. She also told him she was a virgin and married him and had a ring to justify it:

1. On his head was a crown,
2. His hair hang long in rings,
3. His eyes like a stream,
4. His face a formal grove,

5. His speech like musky herbs,

6. His legs were shapely,

7. His palace was swek.

After Menelik showed war strength in the arena, killing a rhinoceros. Queen Madeka announced her son heir to the throne:

1. Tamrin was fascinated,

2. Her minister took position and Madeka buried him Jewish style. Inscription read "No Sun or Moon", God style, "before noon".

Madeka let Solomon set up native churches in Africa, quadrangular and circular. The "Holy Of Holies" always stood in the centers and contained an Ark. At the Cathedral at Axum is the original Ark from Solomon's Temple, which is freely used by laymen and a place of entertainment for travelers (Orr 1955).

Solomon's throne, which was once the guardian of the Ark, is now its exponent. His palace was decorated with personal and royal conduct. It was un-supported by any depended court civilization. Even at Gonda (a city northwest of Ethiopia), the emperors drew their countries to their way of life. But in Ethiopia the emphasis was placed on a form of inimitable stylized conduct. Ten rock churches were built at Lallibela, and the Frescoes at Chennate, Mariam with Egyptian Coptic inspiration

For Church work of high characters of spiritual ancestry, the Ark Of Sion at Axum, locked within seven caskets, is a strong symbol (a treasure house) and the manuscripts also remained in there. A maintained development of schools, all education was theological. There was no renting of the veil.

As time marched on, many forms prevailed; both static and immoral manners sometimes were severe and always tranquil. The laymen mirrored the conception of a providential order of kinship that was Godly inspired. The celestial throne was not maintained by force of arms.

Every empire runs the risk of the development of a shogunate. In Ethiopian History, the record of the emperors at Gondar implies this truth as later sovereigns of that house sunk through a crack. The main slay of the kingdom and the cause of reverence in the Christian subjects kept it together. The individual emperors became discernible. The sage, the Macabeans and the Saints, attached a measure to each one of the supreme Christian Justifications. The Muslims powerfully modified cretin externals of the Ethiopian Kingdomship, but they could attain so that strange personal expression of intangibility. The Chronicles give full details of the wars, which characterized the different renal years. The king always led his men in battle, and there was always a great officer to whom it will "to represent the King in battle". This rule remained until World War II in the United States.

Menelik reassembled the four subordinate kingdoms, especially Madeka with the royal signs, manners, customs, societies, sense of relationship, and obligation, all changed.

Christianity was always fixed at Exum. And it bequeathed the Amharic Mind. When Saint Fruments went to Ethiopia as Bishop, he found stone houses, wattle huts and great syamones of the Old Capital. It was the traffic coming down from Egypt, which led to the foundation of Christian Communities at the seaport (Red Seaport). Saint Frumentius appeared to have converted the Asumite King in the second quarter of the 4th century.

Our knowledge of he regime of Axum is fragmentary; there was a time there was a Hellenists veneer and a Greek coinage. The next factor in Ethiopian History was the rise of Islam, which was submerged by Christian Nubian Kingdom by the tide of this new military faith. By 634 B. C. it was in the hands of the Moslems. The next six centuries witness the gradual Christianization of the plateau and also defense against invading Moslems (Simoons 1960).

In the Cave of Suliman Mountain in Silamdas Karaal, countless diamonds were stored in there. Gold was also stored in there ready to be crushed. Let him who comes follow the map and climb the snowy mountain of Sheba's breast until he comes to the nipple, on the north side of which the great road Solomon made, from the day's journey to the King's place, Let him kill Googol, pray for his soul, farewell, by Jose Da Silvestra. *Is this a direct quote? If so, it should be in quotation marks. Thanks!*

Silvestra himself named the cave Sheba's Breast. Silvestra was a political refugee, a Portuguese who died trying to get to that cave. His stave found him dead and buried him. He wrote this while dying of hunger. The map was given to Delagoa to take to Sir Henry of England in the year of 1590 in Mashulumbwe

Country. Sir Henry set out to find the treasure. On his journey he came in contact with Umbopas looking like a slave tribe, klipringer antelopes, and other animals. The Kaukaunas took the sailing party to the king to be checked out.

Sgagga, their king, joined them on Solomon's great road. They reattached the mine only to find a beautiful old city within its walls, having all columns, huge apartments, skeletons of many imposter, and mummies of the last 15 kings of the Kaukauna. Sir Henry found uncut diamonds, gold, which had Hebrew characters stamped on it, and a collection of elephant tusks. The crew was reduced to three men because of murdering each other. Sir Henry returned to England (Haggard 1957).

HOW CHRISTIANITY WAS SPREAD FROM THIS UNION

The Church in Abyssinia—The Kings of Axum claimed to be descendants from Menelik, son of Solomon. Axum had a rich capital and its ancient sacredness was so great from that period clear down to the 19th century. The kings of Abyssinia would travel there to be crowned. Frumentius 330 A.D. was the first to introduce Christianity, and later was himself consecrated by Saint Athanasuis of Alexandria as the first metropolitan of Ethiopia, taking as his title (Father of Peace).

Beliefs and Practices: creeds, rituals, and practices, the Abyssinian Church agrees generally with copic:

1. Sacraments and prayers for the dead, seven of them,
2. High honor is paid to Mother Mary and to the Saints,
3. Feasts, fasts, and pilgrimages are in such favor,
4. Adults were baptized by immersion and infant by effusions,
5. Christian Sabbath was kept sacred,
6. The Clergy could marry before but not after ordination,

7. The priests were required to read and write and recite the Nicene Creed (Apostle Creed),

8. Conducted ceremonial purification,

9. The Deacons were required to read and prepare Communions.

The Ancient Churches were often Basilican. The Holy of Holies always stood in the center. Tradition declares that the Ark in the Cathedral at Exum could have been the original Ark from Solomon's Temple. European and Egyptian influences are here. The services consist of chanting Psalms, reading scriptures and reciting Liturgies.

The name Abyssinia came from the Portuguese and signifies that the people were of many tribes. Ethiopia was isolated from other countries and relapsed into a primitive half-barbarous civilization. Christianity regained its power in the 14th century. The first followers of Jesus formed a Community or Society at Jerusalem very shortly after Crucifixion of their Master. In the year 65 an organization was founded at Antioch. In Syria, which assumed the name of Christians, and the teachings of Christianity were soon spread throughout the provinces of the Roman Empire by traveling Apostles of whom Saint Paul was perhaps the most famous. Christian societies were organized in the first century in Palestine, Asia Minor, and South Africa. By the beginning of the 4th century, fully one third of the inhabitants of the Eastern World had embraced the Christian Faith, including the Roman Empire and its official support by Emperor Constantine gave it a boost. There were missionaries that visited all parts of the known world, including Asia and the Americas. It finally became the dominant faith of the Western World, never to be serious challenged except for a time by the Islamic moors in North Africa and Spain.

In 1955 there were 741,000,000 Christians in the world, of which some 421,000,000 were Roman Catholics, 127,000,000 Orthodox (Greek) Catholics, and 193,000,000 Protestants. The most numerous of the Protestants Sects were Lutherans, Calvinists and Anglicans, in the order named.

From 2 Chronicles 9:1, the narrator reiterates that God's will is that Solomon executed justice, love, and righteous. The mention of God's will is especially poignant in the light of the illusions else where in the report to the desire of Solon or the desire of the Queen of Sheba.

She was so impressed by his brilliant health and luxury scenery of his palace and at the same time her domain was wealthier than his (without jealousy). After looking around she thought his wealth had exceeded the report she had heard. The exciting news she had heard and read of the coming of Jesus Christ would be a similar report. I believe the brilliancy of his face would have been enough. ("My prayers would be answered, because what follows would be in a palace").

What Queen Madeka did not know was that Solomon had prayed that the glory of the temple might turn the minds of foreign visitors to "know thy name and fear thee". A test of the temple power was given in the case of the Queen of Sheba (1 Kings 8:43). She cried praise Jehovah, but she did not take him home to herself (Langhbaum 1989).

Jesus Christ is unmistakable linked to the line of Solomon, a man the same color. The people, the people were given the Ark of the Covenant by God's own angels. (Daniel 11:40 says near the end when the Messiah comes to Edom, Moab, and Ammons sons will be saved. Libyans and Cushities will be at his feet. Destruction will come to all unsaved people, Gentiles and Jews alike.)

All Ethiopians know that they are descendants of Queen Madeka and the Monarchs that followed her, like the acts and wisdom. Howbeit, I do not believe their words. Blessed be the Lord Thy God because Thy God loved Israel, to establish Thou forever. Therefore God made him King over them, to do judgment and justice. They exchanged gifts to one's desire.

This period of the United Monarchy in I Kings 10:1-13. II Chronicles 9:1-12 says the truth of the matter, talks about Cushities, in the ancient biblical world. Most slaves would have been what are called Caucasians rather than Negroes.

Queen Madeka, King of her homeland was Arbia Felix. Very little was known about him and her until a century ago. A few biblical phrases shred light on them. Roman tales have approved to been founded and the Arab-Traditions have been largely discredited (Zodervan 1997).

The Bible sees Sheba as a symbol of the true Church in the person of Solomon or in the wood of the cross over which she stumbles.

After touring Solomon's domain Queen Madeka said, "Blessed be the Lord Thy God" (I Kings 10:9).

Many legends say Madeka had an affair with Solomon; bore a son, Menelik, who migrated with his followers to the House of Abyssinia, Ethiopia. Her visit was the most romantic love story in history and was passed down even to Jesus' time (Matthew 12:2; Luke 11:31). Madeka's spiritual possibilities made her accept the religion of unity and truth. She was from a people with no faith (Deen 1955).

With the respect to the Queen of Sheba, she had been regarded as reigning over the region embracing land from India to Ethiopia. Most modern writers view her, to the extent that she was an actual historical personality, as a ruler in Southwest Arabia. Interestingly, Josephus saw her as the Queen of Egypt and Ethiopia. Most probably, her domain included territory in both Southwest Asia and Africa. Wherever her location, however, she must be included in the Black Presence, and she was regarded as such, by the example, by Origen. In commenting upon Origen's view, Frank Snoweden writes:

The Queen of Sheba, according to Origen's interpretation of the passage from 1 Kings, by her visit to Solomon provides an important parallel to the person of the Church, whom comes to Christ out of the Gentiles In fulfillment? Of the type represented by the Queen of Sheba, an Ethiopian, the Church comes from Gentiles to hear the Wisdom of King Solomon, and the true lover of peace. When this black and beautiful queen had seen all amazement. But to Origen concludes, when she went to the heavenly Jerusalem, she saw numberous of wonders and considered them splendid.   *Is this highlighted portion a direct quotation from Frank Snoweden? If so, we need to put it in quotation marks. Thanks!*

This period lasted roughly from 922 to 722 B.C. References to a specific Black presence during these years are located in historical records within the biblical books of I and II Kings. This is was an event and oracles that pertained to Egypt and Ethiopia, primarily.

In II Kings 14:25 ff; II Chronicles 12:ff, there was an invasion of Judah by Shish, Pharaoh of Egypt. According to the Chronicles, his army included Libyans, Sukkins, and Ethiopians. One Zeran, the Ethiopian, invaded Judah during the reign of King Asa. Finding no other reference to an Ethiopian ruler with that name, scholars have identified him in many ways. Some speculate that he was an Arabian Chieftain, Kind, or leader from Cushan in Arabia; others postulate that he was an army officer over an occupation force left in Canaan by Shishak. Still another suggests he was a bona fide Ethiopian who was permitted by Pharaoh Osorkon Ist to pass throughout Egypt (Frank M. Swowden).

CHRISTOLOGY

James Orr said he thought King Solomon also told the Queen of Sheba that "a messiah was to come from the seed of David". He was to come of the downfall of the Armenians, to overthrow the Roman in turn. And she asked who may they be? He replied they were the Jewish people that were loyal to Jerusalem even when the national life and religion seemed at their lowest. They were war-like families that divided the nation fractions. They were also un-united and fought disloyalty at home, as well as abroad. They withstood the paganizing influence of the Macedonians and Syrian periods.

John	Judas	Aristobulus	Hyancus
Simeon	John Hyrcanus 135-105	Antigonus	Asamonaews
Judas	Matthias	Alexander	Hashmon
Maccabeus	Jannaeus	Simeon	John
Eleazar	Wife Alesandre	Aristobl	Matthias
Jonathan 140-143	Daughter Wife of Ptolemus	2 Sons	(Orr 1915)

SOLOMON'S WISDOM HOW HE PREACHED TO THE QUEEN

CANANON	1. The lot of the wicked and of their children is a miserable existence. Be happy through virtuous childlessness, secured immortality before guilty parenthood. Though the wise die early, yet they have rest in their death. And accomplish their life mission in the allotted time then they shall see and envy the prosperity of the righteous. Though they shall pass tracelessly away, the righteous shall rejoice in a life that is endless; kings ought therefore to rule according to wisdom and thus attain to immortality.

2. All men come into the world with the same university need of wisdom, which leads to true kingship and immortality. He

pays for wisdom, the main thing and abstaining it had along with every goof thing including knowledge of its kind. He said wisdom depends on all the heroes of Hebrew History from the first man. Adam's time was compared to the Israelites at the Red Sea and in the wilderness.

3. He also taught her theology, anthropology, deontology, hematology, soteriology and eschatology

Theology: The study of God; God is incomparably powerful and omnipresent. All loving, he made the world out of formless matter. The highest conception of creation is the conversion of Shoal into Cosmos. The sufferings of the Israelites were purely penal. What God does was done in the spirit. Which is present everywhere. It also acts as a mediator between God and his creatures and that is a fact. He is all-powerful, sees all things, pervades all things, an influence of the Glory of God, teaches sobriety, understanding, righteousness and courage.

Anthropology means the doctrine of man. Man's soul is breathed into the body and taken back by God. Solomon knew he had a good soul, so he planned to take an undefiled body. A man by nature is evil, his wickedness being inborn. But if he sins it is his own affair, for he is free. And punishment he receives from judicial system is just; it is possible for a person to pass from one class to another.

Deontology means the study of moral obligation of the offerings and sacrifices that he had made every six months. They were made of incense and animals.

Genesis 2:7

Hematology means spiritual death. Spiritual death enters into the world. Sin is made to have its routes in idolatry meaning all sin consists in not giving proper heed to the true God and the moral monstrosities of his time were outgrowths of idolatrous worship.

Soteriology means the study of doc-salvation through Christ. Can wisdom save a man? Immortality to wisdom, all who give heed to the commands of wisdom have the assurance of incorruption and corruption that brings men to God. The knowledge of God's power is the root of immortality.

Eschatology is the doctrine of individuality. Man was created for corruption. The righteousness have a full hope of immortality. Where the wicked died, they had no hope since they suffered in their sins in this present world, as well as in that world which is to come.

God owns everything in this world; all chemicals, all water products, all earthly products, even us (dust), and he did a good job on balancing them. We finally learned to recycle (Delitzsch 1680).

Abyssinia originated with an invading tribe (the Habashats). A Christian kingdom of the 9th and 10th centuries, and they were not restricted to the Northern Fringe of the Highland, as Axum has been, but were located in the very heart of the Ethiopian Plateau. The Abyssinian Kings were at war constantly with the Agow Tribes whose lands they had entered and who more than once menaced the existence of the kingdom. Indeed in the 12th century, an Agow Christian group seized power for a while and moved the capital south to their homeland of Lasta, to establish a new dynasty known as the Zagwe Dynasty. The Zagwes were apparently energetic propagators of the faith, both as missionaries and as builders of churches and monasteries. The most remarkable enterprise of the Zadwes was the construction at Lalibela of Rock-Hewn Churches, which stand today, and which are the central parts of the Pilgrimage Center.

While the Zagwes were converting pagan Agows to Christianity in Northern Ethiopia, Moslems were converting lowland tribes along the Red Sea to Islam and moving into central Ethiopia to slaves, and Moslem colonies were established even in the Christian part of the plateau,

With the consolidation of the Abyssinian Christian State Provinces, especially after the accession to power of a "Solomonic Dynasty" claiming descent from Solomon and the Queen of Sheba, it began to expand southward over Moslem regions, and long struggle broke between Christians and Moslems, apparently not so much because of religious zeal but from the pressure of territorial expansion. The shift of the capital of Abyssinia from Lasta into the country of Amhara confirms the orientation of the emergent stable which, unlike Axum. Looked to its southern marches and not to the Red Sea for military adventures and political expansion (Matthew 1:6-7). Matthew lists Solomon as one of Jesus' ancestors.

The Queen of Sheba (Madeka) heard from the King's lips, but from his eyes, blessed by Jehovah by God, who delighted in thee. Considering the speaker, this statement was not inconsistent with the polytheism. The queen was not willing to admit the existence of the God of Israel on the level of other deities. This means she had become a proselyte to the Hebrew faith and would be claiming too much (Matthew 12:42). She gave to him $3,500,000.00, stones and spices. They were very costly gifts from an opulent Queen (Pfeiffer, Charles).

Alvarez described the Queen of Sheba as a royal lady. Kassa became the Emperor Theodore and became the new Constantine of the Holy Empire of Abyssinia of the ancient Ethiopia "the elect of God for your salvation" (Simmeons 1960).

Judah—when it fell, the Ark of the Covenant disappeared. In the National Geographic Book there was an article that said the Ark might be hidden in a Church and was well guarded (speculation).

Constantine 1—Flavius Valerius Auerlius Constantine "the Great" 288?-337, born in Egypt, a soldier in Egypt and Persia under Diocletian and Galerus.

Constantine in the East

Galerus in the West

Maximan and Manetius were in the West. Constantine was in the East. A draw in Timber, Constantine extended Rome in triumph and adapted The Edict of Milan, after Licinius took to the East and proclaiming Christianity throughout the empire. He devoted himself to the correction of abuses and public extravagance and had a military backup.

Conflict broke our between the East and the West.

He declared himself soul ruler of the Roman world.

He moved his capital to Byzantium in 330A.D. He executed his son for treason and then he had his wife killed for pressing paganism. He banned paganism from his capital. He professed Christianity and allowed himself to be baptized; he also divided the Roman Empires' deed between his sons.

Saint Augustine was one of the greatest theologians that ever lived, born in Numidia in Africa November 13, 354 and died August 28, 340 A.D. Educated in Madaura and Cathage, sent to Milan to teach Rhetoric in 396. He was converted to Christianity and became the Bishop of Hipps, in North Africa for 35 years.

His writings are:
Remarks on the Four Gospels.
The City of God, Confessions, Epistles.

In Ethiopia disciples went and form churches in Rome to conquer the world. St Augustine's body was taken to Rome from Algeria and made a Saint and was painted white. In Palestine in the first century this new faith "Christianity" was the religion based on the teachings of Jesus Christ.

In 1970—There was a group of Black Jews that were airlifted out of Ethiopia to Jerusalem. They spoke Hebrew and practiced Jewish traditions and had a full knowledge of the Torah of Moses. They dressed in American attire, more ancient than Israel herself. Jalah was their classification (this article appeared in Norfolk, Virginia *Pilot* newspaper).

WHY THE QUEEN OF SHEBA (MADEKA) WAS CALLED THE QUEEN OF SHEBA

Although Solomon of Jerusalem was considered the wisest of the East, the Queen of the South was very possibly wiser in wisdom and impregnated the West to the High Dams of Sabaea in the East. Kings and queens from all over the East went to visit and browse. Archaeologists found chariot stables, copper foundries and a shipbuilding city in the middle of a desert. Sheba (Madeka) counted her wealth in trees (watched them grow and finally died and never moaned), stones, waters, and properties of wood, herbs, perfume, medicine and spices. She had knowledge of birds, men, fasting, feasting, copper, glass, wine, forks, and safety pins. She understood jewels and gems, and had a Solomon's mine to stored gold and silver.

The United States describes Sheba as a misty imaginary non-linear and a Sheba consciousness in part of a Black Cultural Renaissance.

The Koran says her throne was stolen, by Solomon, describes her as a sun worshipper, and favors Solomon over David. It also tells of a trick to show hairy legs and love is necessary for work

The Gospel of Matthew calls he the Queen of the South. Thank God she existed. I believe credit should be bestowed to us.

Ethiopia says she built obelisks and temples around the old city of Axum, and she made it the mighty empire at the time of the Trojan War.

The Cabala says she will destroy Rome at the end of time. She was the Queen of the South than whomever Solomon was not wiser.

In 1955—The Ethiopian Constitution declares their kings to be descendants from Solomon and Madeka almost has the character of an inter-government paternity suit.

Josephas referred to her as Nikaulis, Queen of Egypt and Ethiopia. Many of the people were required to live in Jerusalem. They were allowed to dwell in their possession "in the cities of Judah" (Nehemiah 11:3). Solomon was the only king in history that abolished the body guides and mercenaries from nearby provinces but hired an extra scribe for publicity. He also hired twelve commissary officers to draw from all provinces to supply his household (Levine 1980).

The land of Sheba (known as Yemen) of Southern Arabia was a colony of Ethiopia during the Queen of Sheba's reign. Though her royal palace existed in Ethiopia, the Queen ruled her kingdom from both territories.

There is not a time when one necessarily needs answers. If one notices the greater challenges in her life were not likely to go away simply because she had an answer. It is the nature of challenge in this time of transformation to challenge one of the best no matter what difficulties one is encountering The challenge is to live fully in the belief that one can be fulfilled and satisfied right now, exactly as one is.

She trusted what was in her heart rather than merely seemed reasonable. There was not a time that Madeka denied reason, but she thought it was a particularly time to experience her own convictions that seemed to go beyond reason. Reason is a tool for maintaining a functional effective consciousness. Reason is one way of responding to the world in which she lived so that one knows where one is in her world. But the journey was to let her know her place in the world. Her journey to visit the king was ultimately to experience recognition of her own possibilities.

We must remember that King Solomon only asked for wisdom so that he could govern his people property, and the expression of his will. The will of the Queen of Sheba was really looking to see what the King owned "the enrichment of the king" (Longhbaun 1989).

She only wanted to prove to herself what was possible, and what she thought was unnecessary. Through her transformative attitude she knew that her conscious was unfolding. Through her conscious, she knew there were no beginnings and no endings, not even expanding stories from messengers. Her belief in herself had a great deal to do with determining her ability to perceive what her opportunities were again; she just simply explored what she thought was impossible (Berry & Smits 1995).

Solomon received revenue from merchants and trades from all of the Arabian Kings, governors of nearby provinces, Ethiopia, Europe India, and Asia, but Africa had more resources, so he played into Madeka's hands.

The Queen of Sheba's place in history was a land in southern regions of the world (New Testament). In Matthew 12:4, Jesus, reproving the Scribes and Pharisees for demanding a sign, told them of this visit of the Queen of Sheba and to King Solomon, "The queen of the South" and that "one greater than Solomon" was even in their presence.

Madeka has heard of Solomon's God "Jehovah" and how it had made fame. Now don't think for one moment she hadn't done her research. Her territory was larger she thought but she saw the colonies that King Solomon drew from voluntarily. It was a match for her; who is this rival? She found the half was not told. She became a believer, finding the moon and the sun were governed by Jehovah (Orr 1915).

A diplomatic mission was no exaggeration of contemporary city level in Palestine. Madeka was fully aware of the wisdom of Solomon. The palace he had built, his table fare, the seating arrangement of his courtiers, while his officers ate his attendants stood, his butlers, and the burnt offerings. He had all of his servants in order in the temple of Yahweh House. His officers stood to listen to his orders and his wisdom was breathless. "The spirit went out of her and returned."

Solomon received $20,000.00 worth of gold annually apart from what accrued from trade with Arabian Kings and local governors. From Sheba he received 120 talents of gold (Chronicles 9:9), an abundance of spices (Originals) like never before, and precious stones, and because of those King Solomon surpassed all kings of the earth in wealth and wisdom. The entire world conferred with Solomon to benefit from the wisdom God had given him. Every visitor took a gift according to Jewish tradition, yearly.

From Cilicia he got horses, from Shephelah he got cedar and sycamore trees, from Egyptians he received horses, silver, and chariots, and Arabian Rulers gave to him commercial agreements (contracts).

Activities of such a character required all kind of arrangements, including alliances and treaties guaranteed by marriages to foreign princesses, which in turn, necessitated. Each brought his tribute vessels of silver and gold, spices, horses and mules, a fixed quantity every year, and was glad to give because they felt blessed (Myers).

There was an emerald that was shaped into a bowl, which the Queen of Sheba had given to King Solomon that Nicodemus used at The Last Supper and Joseph of Arimathes used the same bowl to catch the blood from the cross founding the order of the Holy Grail.

Emeralds were found in the mountains of Ethiopia, Egypt, Cyprus, and Syria. It also was the third jewel in the first row of Aaron's Breastplate.

Some scriptures that talked about stones were:

1. (2 Chronicles 9:9) Precious stones,
2. (Ezekiel 27:16) Syria with emeralds,
3. (Ezekiel 28:13) Emeralds from the Garden of Eden,
4. (Ezekiel 28:17) The beauty of them.

The New Testament presents us with the Queen of the South (Basililla Rotou) (Matthew 12:42) (Luke 11:31), The Queen of Sheba. She became an eschatological figure who will rise up and condemn the faithlessness of Israel at the final judgment. It is revealing that the New Testament merely call her the Queen of the South, omitting any reference to the land of Sheba, because the same omission is found in Josephus' extensive account of this person, whom he refers to as the Queen of Egypt and Ethiopia, both original, and Jerome considered this Queen as a recast as an eschatological sign against those of his Jewish contemporaries he chastised as being a faithless generation.

There were no priests in Arabia. In Abyssinia among the reins, the inscriptions of Sheba and her son can be found. All Black women were from The Nile Valley (Felder 1989).

RULERS OF ETHIOPIA

KINGS AND QUEENS

MENES (3100 B.C.—3038 B.C.)

TUTHMOSE III (1501—1447)

HALSHEPSUT (1478——1457)

AKHENATON (1375—1358)

TUTANKHAMEN (1361—1343)

MADEKA (960 B.C.—930 B.C.) SOLOMON'S WIFE, THE QUEEN OF SHEBA

DAHIA AL KAHINA 667 B.C. —702 A.D. DESCENDANS OF SOLOMON AND MADEKA

PIANKHI (753—713)

TAHARQA (688—622)

MASSINISSA (202—148)

JUGURIHA (118—106)

GUDIT (937—977)

MANS MUSA I (1312—327)

SUNNI ALI BER (1464-1492)

ASKIA MUHAMMAS (1493—1528)

AFFONSO I (1506—1528)

NZINGHA (1623—1663)

OSEI TUTU (1695—1717)

SHAKA (1813—1829)

MOSHESH (1824—1870)

YAA ASANTEWA (1863—1923

NENELIK II (1889—1913) BLOOD TIES TO SHBA'S SON

HAILE SELASSIE (1930—1974) 111th DESCENDANT OF SOLOMON AND MADEKA.

KINGS

MENES (MENS) (3100 B.C.—3038 B.C.)

Menes ruled Dynasty I (Five Kings) and one of the three dynasties that made up the early dynastic period which flourished from about 3100 B.C.-2513 B.C. The Pharaoh was not a mortal but a God made in man's image. He was a bridge between the Divine forces and his subjects. This means he adapted the characteristics of Egyptian Kings; ancient Memphis is added to his credit. Memphis became a central and leading city; its ruins are near Cairo.

The date of his birth or death is unknown and it is documented that he reigned for sixth years and was killed by a hippopotamus.

Egypt was one of the greatest civilizations of all times and Menes was the most influential ruler in the history of mankind. Pyramids were built; the largest one was built in Gaza for Pharaoh Cheops, 450 feet high.

Egyptians were very serious about their religion, which was polytheism, the belief in many gods. Those gods were represented with heads of animals on human bodies. The chief god of Egypt was the sun god, Ra.

TUTHMOSE III (1501-1447)

Menkheperne Tuthmose III inherited the throne at 10 years of age, and his mother Queen Pharaoh Makare Hatspheput served as his helper. He reigned until his death in 1447 B.C.

There was an establishment of a legal code. There was a project of building magnificent temples, and a great military force, which conquered the southwestern part of Asia and Megiddo from Assyrian rulers, which he took all the spoils (horses, war chariots, cattle and other animals). He even brought Nubians under his control, and used Egyptians as Slaves.

He put his son in line for Kingship, a year later he died, and was thought to have been the greatest military figure in History. His mummy was taken to the Cairo Museum.

HALSHEPUT (1478 B.C.—1458 B.C.)

When Halsheput became the Pharaoh; her mother stole the throne from her, the child Pharaoh, in a coup d'état and proclaimed herself as the Pharaoh and that destroyed her. When the daughter of Tuthmose I became ill, he married her, the princess of her half brother, Tuthmose II. When her father died she became Queen, and one of his sons became the Pharaoh. In a bloody battle Halsephut became the first female Pharaoh in Egyptian History. She swore she was sired by the ancient sun God Amon-Ra and wore male attire.

She erected monuments, engineering, manpower, equipment, equipment, and materials in gold and silver and beautiful temples. She also continued her father's policies, strengthening military defenses and boosted the economy with foreign trade, and she went on to conquer Lower Egypt.

Her reign was 21 years from 1478 B.C.—1457 B.C. Upon the death of her daughter, she designated her stepson/nephew Tuthmose III as her heir. She died at his hand; he attempted to destroy her memories by destroying her monuments. She was the first woman in history to be a female Pharaoh in Egypt's history according to James Henry.

AKHENATON (1375—1356 B.C)

Amehetop IV, known as Akhenton, is renowned for monotheism in Egypt. By worshipping the sun God Aton, he sparked a revolutionary change in the arts. Architecture and literature made a change; the change was known as the Amara Age. His wife was Queen Nefertite. He established worship of Aton and destroyed the temples and the names of his father and removed his capital of Egypt from Thebes to Amara, the modern city of Telemarna.

He was interested in the arts and needed no security to roam the streets. He respected women and his family. His religious reforms and his loss of Egyptian respect caused interval conflicts. The people referred to him as "The Criminal", and he died at the age of 31 and the people returned to polytheism (many gods).

Nefertiti (the beautiful one) was admired for her dress "Ruler of the Nile". She was the wife of Pharaoh Akhenaton, influenced by establishing monotheism, worshiping the sun god, Aton. Matched her husband in religious nature, praying of divinity while her husband was still alive. She had her name put in stone on the building, which stirred the people.

She was the mother of six children (daughters). A good mother always embraced her kids. Her husband died and she married the son of the King of the Hittites. The prince died en route to Egypt. One of her daughters ascended the throne. Her picture is in the Museum in Berlin.

TULANKHAMEN (1361—1343 B.C.)

Tulankahamen was an Egyptian king of the 18th dynasty. His tomb was discovered (1922) almost in tact near Thebes, yielded furniture and other funerary objects of great splendor throwing light on the art and life in Ancient Egypt.

He was 19 years old and died early. A young statesman succeeded him. Thebes became an abandoned city and he died of a wound in his ear (from a hemorrhage in battle). Toys and food were placed in his coffin.

Of all the religious ideas of the Egyptians, their belief in a life after death has left the most lasting evidence. They buried their dead as mummies in pyramids with all they needed in the next life. The Egyptians also included with each body a papyrus roll containing prayers and charms, which would be useful to the departed soul.

MAKEDA (960 B.C.—(30 B.C.)
"THE QUEEN OF THE SOUTH"
"TO THE MOSLEM, SHE WAS BILQUIS"

She was the Queen of Ethiopia and Saba. Axum was the capital of her empire, 100 years after the great flood.

Makeda made many changes, and rebuilt the territory of Sheba. She was beautiful and very wealthy. Her visit to Solomon is in the Kings and Chronicles books of most Bibles. Giving him so much, and she was impressed with his wisdom. Her six-month visit made her give up her religion and adopted Judaism. Solomon preferred her to remain even though he had many wives. Solomon gave her a ring so she would not forget him. Queen Makeda promised King Solomon if she delivered a male child she would crown him King of Ethiopia and promise was magnificent. She returned home, and 9 months and 5 days after Makeda left King Solomon, she gave birth to a male child and named him Menelik.

HAILE SELASSIE (1930—1974 A.D.)
(RAS TAFFARI MAKONNEN)

Selassie was born in Harar, Ethiopia in 1928. He was named King on November 2, 1930, he was crown emperor. He lost his throne in 1936, when the Italians in an unprovoked attack overturned his country. In the course of World War II, British forces drove out the Italians at Adowa 1940-41, and Haile Selassie resumed his throne, and believed to have been the 111th descendant of King Solomon and Sheba (Madeka).

In 1907 he modernized the government; in 1916, Ethiopia remained neutral during World War 1. Ethiopia became a member of The League of Nations (Empak).

HOW CHRISTIANITY WAS SPREAD FROM THIS UNION

SUMMARY

Many stories can be developed from this story. Readers can dwell on adultery, betrayal, incest, family conflict, rivalry, and envy, indentured servants, a traitor brother, a greedy father of unjust and soft-hearted judges, treasure hunters, and crafty merchants, angry kings, imprudent workers and obsessive gardeners, clever inventors, feats and parties, wars and marriages, life and death.

Stories of God are designed to discern, to open to the power of God's chocking love and to disclose to us new ways of living in the world with the illumination and power that comes with love.

It also shows us how God reacts and behaves with those who bargain with him, by demanding favors to which they have earned rights through their own good deeds. We win his mercy and forgiveness through our efforts.

This story can be bound together, using the symbols or "sacraments" to reveal the presence of grace from Jesus the Christ. The sacraments were water, wind and spirits, beasts (food and drink), light, an open door, women (many women) showing how God acts and for that matter what the Church ought to be.

The statue: Man and woman are equal! It is a flinty knife and woman has to accept it. Madeka (The Queen of Sheba) helped Solomon to know there was another wise person in the world as well as himself. Man is an upper-handed animal. If he suffers an unfortunate loss and keeps his accumulation in his pocket. He should tear up all of his losses and won't defeat his own purposes. What he doesn't realize is the weight of its purpose. He can extinguish candles and relight them again.

REFERENCES

BUDGES Wallis E, A., —THE QUEEN OF SHEBA AND HER ONLY SON ME-NEDELEK 1922, THE KEBRA NEGAST, BY OXFORD UNIVERSITY PRESS, LONDON

BERRY, HALLE, AND JIMMY SMITS, —- SOLOMON AND SHEBA 1955

BUSBY, MARGARET, —DAUGHTERS OF AFRICA 1994, BY BALLENTINE PUBLISHERS, NY.

COLEMAN, WILLIAM, —TODAYS' HANDBOOK OF BIBLICAL TIMES AND CUSTOMS 1984.BY BETHANY HOUSE PUBLISHERS

DEEN, EDITH, —ALL THE WOMEN OF THE BIBLE 1955,BY HARPER AND ROW, SANFRANCISCO CALIFORNIA

DEITZSCH, (IRIS), —1680, PAGE 116-127 KORAN XXVVII

EMPAK INC., —1998-2003, BY EMPAK PUBLISHERS CHICAGO, ILL

FELDER, CAIN HOPE, —TROUBLING BIBLICAL WATERS 1989,BY ORBIA BOOK PUBLISHERS' MARYNOL N.Y.

GRAY, JOHN, —I & II KINGS 1970, BRIGHT HISTORY LIBRARYP 118, BY PHILADELPHIS, WESTMINISTER

GRISPINO, JOSEPH A., —THE CHILDRENS' BIBLE 1965,BY GOLDEN PRESS, N.Y

GUTHRIE, D. & MOLYER, J. A., —THE NEW BIBLE COMMENTARY REVISED, 1953

HAGGARD, RIDER H., —SHEBA AND SOLOMON MINES 1957,PUBLISHER RADOM HOUSE IN U.S. BY WOLF

HENDELSON, WILLIAM H., —THE NEW WORLD FAMILY ENCY. 1957, BY PUBLISHERS STANDARD INTERNATIONAL LIBRARY INC. N.Y.C.

HOUSMAN, GERALD, —THE SHELDON STORY OF READING PLEASURE, THE KINGS 1997, KEBRA NAGAST BY ST. MARLIN PRINTERS, N.Y.

ISLEN, FEDERICK CARL, —THE ABINGDOM BIBLE COMMENTARY

1929, BY ABINGDOM PRESS, NASHVILLE TENN.

LANGHBAUM, J.S., —THE NEW INTERPERTERS' BIBLE, 1989 PUBLISHER ABING PRESS, NASHVILLE TENN.

LEVINE, FAYE, —SOLOMON AND SHEBA 1980, PUBLISHER RICHARD AND ST MARTINS

LOCKER, HERBERT, —NEW ILLUSTRARED BIBLE DICTIONARY 1995 PUBLISSHER NELSON, NASHVILLE TENN.

LONENZ KONRAD, —KING SOLOMONS' RING 1997, PUBLISHER HARPER AND ROW, N.Y.

MC AULIFF, DAMMEN JANE, —DEMONIZING THE QUEEN OF SHEBA, 1999, VOL. 58, P 229, VIA-INTERNET

MILLER, LANE &MADELINEM, —THE NEW HARPERS BIBLICAL DIC-TIONARY, 1955, P 630

MYERS, JACOB M., —INVITATION TO THE OLD TESTAMENT, 1967 PUBLISHED BY DOUBLEDAY AND COMPANY GARDEN CITY, N.Y.

ORMONE, CZENZI, —SOLOMON, SOLOMON AND THE QUEEN OF SHEBA, 1913, PUBLISHER, FARRAR STRUS ANDYOUNG, N.Y.

ORR, JAMES, —THE INTERNATIONAL STANDARD BIBLE ENCY., 1915, PUBLISHER, THE HOWARD CORP. CHICAGO, ILL.

PFEUFFER, CHARLES F., —THE WYCLIFF BIBLE COMMENTARY, PUB-LISHER MOODY PRESS, CHICAGO, ILL.

POYNTER, EDWARD, —THE VISIT OF QUEEN SHEBA TO KING SOL-OMON, 1884-90, BY ART GALLERY, SOUTH WALES, PICTURE IN OIL ON CANVAS

SAFRA, JACOB E., —THE QUEEN OF SHEBA, 1998, THE BRITANNIA, PRINTED IN CHICAGO, ILL.

SHEFFIELD PRESS, —THE STUDY OF THE OLD TESTAMENT, NO.75 1990, BY SHEFFIELD PRESS

SIMOONS, FEDERICK J., —ETHIOPIA-PEOPLE AND ECONOMY, 1960, PUBLISHER, UNIVERSITY PF WISCONSIN PRESS, MADISON, WISCONSIN

SIMS, ABERT E, & GEORGE DENT, —WHOS' WHO IN THE BIBLE, 1992, PUBLISHER CASTLE BOOKS, SECAUCUS, N.J.

SNOWEN, FRANK M., —BLACKS IN ANTIQUITY, 2005PUBLISHER BEKNAP AT HOWARD UNIVERSITY PRESS

WILLIS, EARNEST A SIR, —MANUSCRUIPT OF ISKAK'S VERSION, 1922, IS IN THE BRITISH MUSEUM OF KEBRA NAGST

ZONDERVAN CORP, —QUEEN SHEBA (MEDAKA), 1997, THE AFRICAN DEVOTIONAL BIBLE, PUBLISHER ZONDERVAN CORP, GRAND RAPIDS, MICHIGAN.

ARTICLES

CHICAGO PRESS, -SUB-JEWISH TRADITION. This article tells of a clever, resourceful, cunning, menacing female who threatened the boundaries of gender. And it draws on a profound and intimate of both Jews and Muslim resources. 1984—over 1,000,000,000 (1 billion) Moslems were in the world that believed that the spirit of lying compounded the curse that had fallen on Ishmael many centuries before. Describing Mohammed's vision:

(Genesis 16:12) A wild ass of a man he will be, against him, sitting to defy in brother. The descendants of Ishmael are the Arabians. Once the lying spirit was uncanned by Mohammed. A different curse was hung around the neck of Ishmael giving him a second one. As that was the anathema or curse of Paul.

(Galatians 1:8) But even if we or an angel from heaven should preach a gospel other than the one we preach to, let his be eternally condemned.

THE DETROIT NEWSPAPER, February 14, 1996 by David C. Butty: An ambassador and representative to the U.N. Mulugeter will unveil an animated figure of the Queen of Sheba at the American Heritage center on Friday. The figure will be on permanent display at the center, 21511 W. Nichols, along with five other displays, including a Kora played from Gamis. The figure will tell the stories of the relationship with the Hebrew leader which produced a son (Menelik) who went to find succeeding dynasties leading to the Emperor of Ethiopia, Haile Selassie.

NOVEMBER 1949, Ralph Bunch, an American Black: Armistice agreements between the various Arab nations and Israel were signed, (Jerusalem Reunition) to remove the Jordanians out.

1951- Zionist Congress—The first one ever held in Israel

1972 -Foreign Missions. Out of 46 foreign missions in Israel 10 of them were Africans (Central African Republic, Congo Brazzaville, Congo Kinshasa, Dehomey Gabon, Ivory Coast, Liberia, Malagast, Niger and Upper Viola).

www.ingramcontent.com/pod-product-compliance
Lightning Source LLC
Chambersburg PA
CBHW052204150726
48002CB00003B/1110